To: A

From: Tashma :)

The Unwed Wife

Step Off the Curb

Publishing, LLC

Published by Step Off the Curb Publishing, LLC
Book design by Derica Curtis of Curtis Services

Printed in the United States of America

ISBN: 978-0-692-96817-8
LCCN: 2019911645

My beloved sister,

The purpose of this book is to remind you to have faith in God, for only He can guide you to the path that leads to that great romance that awaits you.

About the Author

Tashma White has volunteered with community service organizations that assist children and women in need since she was ten years old. Some thirty years later, she continues to serve, but with a focus on kingdom building for the Lord. Ms. White is a member of Delta Sigma Theta Sorority, Inc. and has a bachelor of science from Appalachian State University in North Carolina with a major in communications. Tashma currently resides in Texas where she's working on her next literary adventure and loves to hear from her readers.

Please feel free to contact her at

www.tashmawhite.com

or follow her on Twitter at @TashmaWhite

What's Next in

The Unwed Wife Series?

The Unwed Wife—Study Guide

The Unwed Life: Survival Guide

Coming Soon!

How to Love Me While Waiting for H.I.M.

(Husband in Marriage)

How to Love Him Without Losing Me

Red Diamond Celebrations:

Cookbook and Entertainment Style Guide

Dedication

"O LORD, you are my God; I will exalt you and praise your name, for in perfect faithfulness you have done marvelous things, things planned long ago."

Isaiah 25:1 NIV

This book is dedicated to the Great El Shaddai (God Almighty). YHWH, You are the first of all my loves. Thank You for making the creation of this book part of my lifelong purpose and for using me as a vessel to bring this vision to life. Lord Jesus, none of this would have ever been possible without You! You bottle my every tear and have never rejected me. Thank You, Most High King. Eternal Sire, You are and will forever be my Heavenly Papa.

Love always,

Your clingy child, Tashma

My "Finish Line"

Acknowledgments

This book has taken years of work, perseverance, time, and discipline. And yet, I confess that this section was the hardest one to write. As I began to ponder who to include, I thought about all of my family and friends, those I love and care for deeply. It would be virtually impossible to list everyone who has influenced me in some way. Hence the reason why I worried if I attempted to name everyone, I would accidentally forget someone important.

Thankfully, the Holy Spirit resolved my dilemma by instructing me to write "Finish Line" acknowledgements. In other words, I was to list only those who prayed and pushed me across the finish line to completing this book. Once my spirit received this divine instruction, the following words poured freely from me. *Thank You, Heavenly Papa!*

First and foremost, all praises and honor belong to the Great I Am for His faithfulness, anointing, and provisions. "*What is impossible with men is possible with God.*" Luke 18:27 NIV.

To my mother, Gail T. White. Mama, it was you who demonstrated a living example for me of having faith in God. All those years of working in a factory, standing for hours on concrete flooring and handling itching materials made out of fiberglass, just so your children could finally have a home of their own. Thank you for loving and taking care of us. I also want to acknowledge that it was you who kept pushing and reminding me through the years to stay focused so that I could finish this book. All praises to the King of all kings, for He blessed me to do just that. And to think, me being a talker was actually good for something after all! Hahaha :-)

To my soul twin sister in Christ, Tammy Camper: you were the first person I shared the vision of *The Unwed Wife* with in 2004, and you've been there with me EVERY step of the way. Through the years, you've kindly read and edited my drafts and literally pushed me forward toward the book's completion. You've prayed me through devastating heartbreaks, hurtful rejections and spiritual strongholds. Furthermore, you know the good, the bad, and the very ugly; and yet, you love me anyway. I want to thank not just you but your wonderful husband, Curt, as well for making me a part of your beautiful family. I love you all very much.

To Rachel Starr Thomson, the most amazing editor with supernatural patience! Thank you for guiding me through this publishing process.

Even more, for taking a wordy, haphazard manuscript and shaping it into the beautifully written document that we see today. Partnering with you on this project has been an incredibly rewarding experience. I am grateful to the Lord for guiding me to you.

To my original team of editors: Gail T. White, Tammy Camper, Sonya Pearson, and Jerri Harris. Thank you, ladies, for humoring me and reading my first draft manuscript. Make no mistake, it all started with you!

A tremendous thanks to Derica Curtis of Curtis Services for bringing my vision of this book to life! I also want to thank you for turning my humdrum blog into a wonderfully designed work of art. Your talents really helped to glide this literary voyage to the next level. Thank you, my friend!

To my pastor and first lady, Dr. Delvin Atchison and Dr. Brenda Atchison, for your generous support of this book. I cannot thank you enough for the sacrifice of your time and inspiring words. Your endorsement of this endeavor means the world to me!

To my brother, Charles "Vernon" White, Jr., and my sweet sister-in-law, Ericka, for your continuous love and support. Love always to you both!

To J.C. Byers, I love you and thank you for adopting me as your daughter. You always seemed to know exactly when I needed some inspiration for writing this book. You are appreciated!

To my cousin, Terrence D. Rucker, a tremendous thanks for always being there and never complaining (at least not to my face… hahaha) when I needed you the most! I love you, Big Cuz.

To my aunt Sheila F. Rucker, for always supporting and encouraging me to be myself. Love you!

To Donya Imes, Kaychele Mcclelland, and Michelle Murdoch: Ever since we were children in school, you three have been some of my most beloved best friends. Thank you for always being there and supporting me. I love you guys now and forevermore!

To Sharlene Brittian for orchestrating my official book launch at Westside Baptist Church.

To the Sorors of Delta Sigma Theta Sorority, Inc. who have and may support this project, I thank you from the bottom of my heart!

To the Bruhs of Omega Psi Phi Fraternity, Inc. at Westside Baptist Church: for supporting me when I needed it most, thank you!

To Maria M. Thurman, thank you for helping me to solidify the concept of the Red Diamond. I love you, Little Sunflower.

To Porscha Bruner, for lifting me and this book up in prayer. I love you, Sis.

To the prayer ministry, The Sista Power Hour

of Prayer: Stacy Cullivan, Zandra Kirvin, Mikita McNeal, Lynn Washington, Tracie Lockett and April Benton. You all are my sisters, and I love each of you very much. I've lost count of how many times you all have prayed for and stood with me in faith about finishing this book. All praises to our Eternal King that it's FINALLY here! Won't He do it? *Oh yes, He did!*

To the Women at the Well prayer ministry: Natalie Walker-Jones, Tina Rosado and Zandra Kirvin (again), our weekly prayers and occasional fasting have helped me with stand one of the most difficult periods of my life. Thank you, ladies, for believing with me about *The Unwed Wife.*

To my aunt Mae and uncle Andrew Johnson, thank you for consistently loving and supporting me throughout the years. I love you both dearly.

To Rodney, Janet and McKenzie DuPree, thank you guys for supporting me and being such great friends. I love you!

To the Women's Ministry at Westside Baptist Church: Thank you for believing in me and supporting this project.

To my Redwoods family: Thank you for being the best Sunday school class at Westside Baptist Church, number three to be exact (wink)! You've prayed and supported me (both spiritually and financially) when I had no one else I could turn to. I will never forget! I love each and every one of you.

To my Master's Touch family at Reid Temple A.M.E. Church: You guys will forever be my original church family. This ministry truly embodies the Spirit of Jesus Christ by feeding those most forgotten, the homeless. I know the Creator of All Things sees your consistent sacrifice and is pleased. Thank you for continuing to inspire me all the way from Maryland! I love all of you and miss you *so* much.

To Christie Moore: Girl, how many times have we cried and declared that we would someday walk in our purpose? It's here, and the best is yet to come! Love you, Sis.

To the Toastmasters at Westside Baptist Church: It was you who gave me the tools to stand and speak with confidence and courage. You have breathe life into my God-given purpose. Thank you!

To LaShawn Bing: For being not only an awesome trainer but a God-fearing mentor as well. Love you, Sis.

To Michelle Turner: Thank you for loving and supporting me in the writing of this book. You're still my adopted Baby Girl!

To Naomi Woodard: Thank you for being there for me, Sis.

To my BGR family: Thank you for beginning my journey to a healthier lifestyle.

To Soror Cassandra Dillon, for revealing a seed that began the planting and growth of this book.

To Mrs. JoEtta Willis and Ms. Elaine Williams: Thank you for your love and support of this book. I am truly grateful and love you both always.

To my "There's No Unwed Wife" blog family: Your support gave me the spark I so desperately needed when I first began to write. Thank you kindly!

To Barbara and John Reliford: For supporting me through the creation of this book and for being true friends, thank you! I love you both dearly.

To Marie Palin: I'm grateful for your encouragement over the years about this book. Can you actually believe it's done? I appreciate you connecting your unwavering faith with mine. Also, thanks for offering to translate this book for me in French. You do know that I'll be calling you soon, right? :-) I love you, Lil Sis.

To my Westside Baptist Church family: I appreciate each person who has and will support this endeavor. I've been shown nothing but love since the very first day I walked through the doors of the sanctuary. Thank you from the depths of my heart!

Dr. Delvin Atchison, Senior Pastor

Westside Baptist Church

"Once or twice in a generation, a book is published that has a simple concept reintroduced with lasting impact. *The Unwed Wife* is just such a book. Tashma White presents a life-altering biblical principle whose profundity is defined by its simplicity. This book creates awareness, promotes recognition, and offers redemption. *A must-read for single Christians and the leaders who minister to them.*"

Foreword

by Dr. Brenda Atchison

When Tashma asked me to write the foreword to this book, I jumped at the opportunity. To that point, my experience with Tashma had been through the Westside Baptist Church Women's Ministry. I had heard her give a very personal and poignant testimony during a women's conference session on standing on God's promises. Her courage and authenticity were riveting. I realized then that Tashma and I shared a similar philosophy and passion concerning women's issues.

After reading the first couple of chapters, I was all in. I felt *The Unwed Wife* embodied both my philosophical leanings and passion to support women with knowledge. I believe when we know better, we do better and consequently we live better. Someone once said, "When you educate a man, you educate an individual; but when you educate a girl, you educate a nation." I am a firm believer in the sanctity of marriage. We are living in a time where the boundaries of marriage have been both blurred and distorted through constant media bombardment. We need the sound doctrine found in *The Unwed Wife*.

Tashma speaks with an authentic and authoritative voice that is convicting, yet nonjudgmental. The idea of dating is elucidated in a manner that explores the pitfalls of being single while claiming the benefits of marriage. In a carefully crafted narrative, she skillfully navigates the terrain of singleness using the overarching theme of relying on God's commandments to receive God's blessings. God's promises can only be secured as we are guided by His principles.

Using lived experiences and poignant examples from Scripture, Tashma explains the missteps and perils of GTWI (giving the wrong impression). She builds her riveting narrative precept upon precept.

—Dr. Brenda Joy Atchison, Professional Business and Life Coach

The Unwed Wife

by

Tashma D. White

Table of Contents

How to Use This Book

1. The Awakening

2. Whose Daughter Are You Anyway?

3. The Eight Types of Unwed Wife

4. The Enemy in the Mirror

5. The Five Main Ingredients to a Woman's Love Life

6. The Four Principles of Courting Versus Dating

7. What Type of Food Are You?

8. So, You've Fallen. Now What?

9. The Fresh Scent of Forgiveness

A Final Note

APPENDICES

Appendix A: Prayers for Today's Single Woman

A Prayer for the Sister Who Wants to Break the Curse of The Unwed Wife Syndrome

The Red Diamond (No Unwed Wife) Pledge

A Prayer for the Sister Who Lacks Self-Awareness

A Prayer for the Sister Who Lacks Self-Respect

A Prayer for the Sister Who Lacks Self-Worth

A Prayer for the Sister Who Has a Fear of Being Alone
A Prayer for the Sister Who Has a Fear of Rejection
A Prayer for the Sister Who Wants to Give Her Life to the Lord
A Prayer for the Sister Who Wants to Be Married Someday
A Prayer for the Sister Who Keeps Choosing Mr. Wrong
A Prayer for the Single Mother Who Longs for a Loving and Faithful Man of God
A Prayer for the Sister Who Is Struggling With Her Finances

Prayers of Healing

A Prayer of Healing for the Divorced Sister in Christ
A Prayer of Healing for the Sister Who Is Having Suicidal Thoughts
A Prayer of Healing and Restoration for the Sister Who Has Been A Victim of Domestic Abuse
A Prayer of Healing for the Sister Who Has Been Sexually Abused

Appendix B: Prayers for Today's Young Lady

A Prayer for the Young Lady Who Wants to Break the Curse of The Unwed Wife Syndrome
The Red Diamond (No Unwed Wife) Pledge

A Prayer for the Young Lady Just Beginning to Date
A Prayer for the Young Lady Who Is Going Off to College
A Prayer for the Young Lady Who Is in School or College
A Prayer for the Unmarried Young Lady With Children

Glossary of Terms

How to Use This Book

The Reflection Pool

~ Your Reflection Pool ~

At important points of each chapter is a tool to help you get the most from this book. A reflection pool is a still body of water created to be calm and reflective. The "Reflection Pools" featured in this book are tools to prayerfully inspire deep insight within you. Whether it's a memory or a new discovery that floats up from the depths of your unconsciousness while you ponder what you're reading, write it in your reflection pool. You will be able to track the progression of your thoughts from beginning to end. If a stronghold surfaces, pray and ask the Lord to grant you the fortitude and self-control needed for deliverance. It's my hope that the Holy Spirit will saturate and flow thoroughly through the pages of this book, so much so that you will receive a lasting imprint of His presence, one that will permeate your body and flow straight to your heart.

Red Diamonds

As a proud member of Delta Sigma Theta Sorority, Inc., I am partial to anything red (our distinguished colors are crimson and cream). I am also fascinated with the science of gems. Never could I have imagined that the Holy Spirit would combine my love of red, or better yet crimson, with my passion for learning about rare stones, but He has, and here's how.

Late one evening, the Lord instructed me to research the world's gems. What I found thrilled me beyond words. I discovered a diamond so extraordinary that if there were a beauty pageant among gems, it would be crowned fairest of them all. True red diamonds (not to be confused with rubies or garnets) are the rarest of all diamonds. Most are found in the Argyle Diamond Mine in Western Australia. According to the Cape Town Museum in Africa, there are only thirty true gem-quality red diamonds known to exist in the world. Out of all the diamond colors in the world, red is the purest, even surpassing blue, orange, pink, purple, and yellow diamonds. Red diamonds are so exquisite that they are priced at hundreds of thousands of dollars *per carat!*

Beloved, the choice to refuse to live the lifestyle of an unwed wife is as rare as the red diamond. It is also one of the most challenging in terms of our spiritual sacrifice. As a result, I've chosen the red diamond as a symbol for the daughter-in-Christ who refuses to live her life as an unwed wife. At the end of every chapter, you will have an opportunity to *collect your red diamond* as a reward for completing the reading. You will be creating your own jeweled garland of wisdom as you finish this book.

1

The Awakening

"Being unable to forgive myself for past sins kept me in bondage, but God's forgiveness freed me and awakened my life's purpose."
—Tashma White

Your life is like a house. The front door is designed to welcome guests. The back door is designed for exiting. There are only two ways to bring folks into your house of life. You can proudly welcome them through the front door for everyone to see. For example, a respected pastor and his wife, invited to dinner—or a cherished friend who's come to say hello. Then there are those you can only bring in through the back door. These relationships are the ones we intentionally go into knowing they are out of the will of God.

I'm talking about the married man with whom we are having an affair. How about that boyfriend who has unlimited access to our body, car, home, and finances? Better yet, how about that pretty boy we desperately want to love us although his actions say otherwise? Or maybe we attract those males who would rather live off a woman than support one. I once heard a pastor say, "There used to be a time when we had pretty women and hardworking men. Now we have hardworking women and pretty men!" On the flip side, it is equally wrong when a woman's only intent is to seek materialistic gain from a man.

Instead of ridding ourselves of the spiritual sewage that results from these bad relationships, we often choose to pollute our lives and spirits by clinging to them. Controlled by our current

Your Reflection Pool

circumstances, we fail to see the possibilities of what God has in store for our future. We lack faith and patience to wait on the man God has custom-made for us.

For years, I expected my soul mate to arrive like a surprise package from FedEx. When my dream delivery never came, I got tired of waiting on God and snuck out to find my own version of happily ever after. You can guess how that turned out—possibly because you've lived the same story, and you're dealing with your own set of consequences because of it.

The good news is that there's help for those of us wandering through the maze of single life. Our own personal Tour Guide is ready and willing to show us the way. *Here's a hint:* Although we can't see Him, He dwells within all of God's children. I'm talking about none other than the *Holy Spirit*. If we are children of God, we are all capable of hearing Him. As Corrie Huyser wrote in her paper *The Person of the Holy Spirit,* we hear with "the part of our mind—the part of our spirit—that is joined with the Mind of God."

Now, you won't hear too many authors saying this, but nonetheless here we go: *this book is not for everyone!* Be warned, the more you read, the less support you will find for today's accepted views on dating. There will be no ringing endorsement for Internet dating services or any other matchmaking methods for hire. Nor will there be a push to rush you into marriage. Quite the contrary! Holy matrimony is too serious to take lightly. Instead, what you will uncover here is constant food for thought as you are prayerfully encouraged to trust and wait on the Lord for your future spouse.

Sure, many of us know that more than 50 percent of marriages end up in divorce. *Imagine, though, what would happen if we truly allowed the Holy Spirit to lead us during the dating process*. I am willing to believe the divorce rate would drastically drop. A lot of unequally yoked marriages would never occur in the first place. *An unequally yoked marriage is where the wife and husband are not spiritually lined up or equal. One is a spiritually minded believer of Jesus Christ while the other is not.* For believers, this can be a major cause of marriage failure.

Overall, the goal of *The Unwed Wife* is to examine the boundaries an unwed daughter of Christ should operate within while in a relationship with a man who is not her husband. You will be encouraged to take a hard look at whether what you are *willing* to provide a boyfriend is similar to what God would *only* expect your husband to receive. I know how difficult it can be to change direction from what's familiar, particularly when it comes to the world of dating. However, if our behavior keeps us in bondage, I'm a witness that we can be set free. I want to empower you with the vision that the Lord gave to me, one that inspired my own decision for freedom. We are

Your Reflection Pool

beloved daughters of the King of kings and are part of a royal priesthood. That's why neither one of us has to settle for someone who will not honor us before our Majestic Father. In chapter 4, we'll explore why this is even important.

No matter what our situation is today, the Holy Spirit is the best relationship expert any daughter of Jesus Christ can ever hope to have! We don't have to worry about Him spreading our business at church, school, or work. We can know beyond any shadow of a doubt that He has our best interests at heart—and that His methods will work. What are accepted forms of payment for His services? Well, certainly not the $25 to $200 per session charged by some couples' therapists. No, His required form of payment will cost you much more than any dollar amount! You simply need to be willing to shut down the strongholds of flesh and pride in your mind in order to receive His anointed counsel. It's a high price, but one you can afford—in fact, you can't afford *not* to pay it.

All we have to do is diligently seek the Lord. We can have access to Him anywhere, anytime. It was in seeking the Lord that I received the powerful awakening I'm attempting to encapsulate in this book, a revelation I call *The Unwed Wife Syndrome*. I received the revelation of this spiritual stronghold after my husband and I decided to end our seven-year marriage. Selfish mistakes made on both of our parts had crumbled the foundation of our wedding vows. Neither of us was willing to admit that we played a starring role in the demise of our union. I had become self-righteous and lacked wifely submission, while he was unforgiving and bitter. (That's what happens when you leave Jesus Christ at church instead of making Him the center of your home.) Then I had the nerve to become shocked when things didn't work out.

Afterward, I went through a spectrum of emotions that ranged from anger to hopelessness. The depression was the most damaging. I gained weight, couldn't sleep, and suffered from anxiety. In my heart, I was convicted for failing to honor my marriage vows, and I had to ask forgiveness for the sin of my divorce. I wasn't healed from this guilt until I repented before the Lord.

On top of that, I shuddered at the thought of going back to the social circus otherwise known as the dating scene. I was no longer the bright-eyed young lady with a tiny waist and flawless skin. I was now a forty-seven-year-old woman with control top pantyhose who grunted and groaned while doing thirty minutes of exercise. If that wasn't enough, nothing had changed about the scene since the last time I dated. In fact, things had grown worse! Now we have to deal with the Down Low brothers. Their shadowy presence is as dangerous to women as a silent stalker. Suffice it to say, my pop-up image of a happy life forever with Mr. Right crashed to the ground like a kite with no wind.

~ Your Reflection Pool ~

Quite simply, I would rather have walked down a runway without Spanx than start dating again!

The change began late one evening while I was in the shower. As I said earlier, I was gifted with a powerful awakening from the Holy Spirit. It allowed me to understand that I simply didn't know how to date as a single daughter of Jesus Christ and how important it was for me to learn. The Holy Comforter helped me to realize that in order to have a blessed union the next time around, I had to start from the beginning—the dating period.

As a divorced woman who hopes to be in love again someday, I knew this was important for me to grasp. A popular definition of *insanity* is *"to perform the same action over and over again while expecting a different result."* Quite frankly, I didn't want to take the same *insane* approach to relationships only to end up with another failed ending. Historically, once I fell in love with a man I gave everything I have to offer. I performed as a wife without the sanctity of marriage, offering sex, cooking, cleaning, around-the-clock access to my time—etc. The Lord knows I didn't seek a true relationship with Him until my marriage fell apart. Now I know that consistently leaning on His guidance is the real secret to the success of a relationship. In addition, I learned that there must be a clear distinction between what we offer as a girlfriend and what we give as a wife.

One day while working on this book, I took a quick break and called Tammy, my cherished friend, to chitchat. After she inquired about my progress, we somehow got on a *"If I knew then what I know now"* discussion on shacking. Tammy began reflecting on dating regrets with her then-boyfriend, now her beloved husband of almost twenty years. She spoke about how she would often spend the night at his house, justifying their behavior because they didn't officially live together until after their wedding.

"It was the same as shacking up," she told

me, *"no matter how I tried to fix it up."* Yet many would simply label it as a woman spending occasional weekends or nights with her boyfriend. My first thought was, *Wow, I never looked at it like that!* Now me, I knew I was guilty as charged. My ex-husband and I had shacked up together before we got married. Even before we started shacking, we spent every weekend at each other's apartment. Talk about an expert in doing everything the wrong way! But like Tammy often says, *"Sin is sin."*

When you think about it, she's absolutely correct. As I reflected on all this, I came to realize that there *are* various forms of shacking up, and the Holy Spirit helped me narrow them down to three. As it turned out, these three forms of shacking up are the perfect jumping-off point for the phenomenon of the unwed wife —so I want to begin our examination of this topic here.

But first, what exactly is shacking? Most people define *shacking* or *shacking up* as *"an*

❧ Your Reflection Pool ❧

unmarried man and woman living together as lovers."

I think it's safe to say that most people are familiar with this version. Now, I'd like to introduce you to two other forms: *short-term shacking* and *giving the wrong impression.*

Short-term shacking is when we temporarily spend the night with a man who is not our husband for the purpose of a close and/or sexual relationship (i.e. one night or occasional weekends). Ladies, staying over at our sweet thang's house for one or several nights a week is just as out of order as living there.

There are also times when we *give the wrong impression (GTWI)* about our personal life. A *GTWI* is committed when we mentally drive through the roadblocks of wisdom and continue down a path that can lead us to self-sabotage. In other words, it is *behaving in a way that could encourage people to question the sincerity of our walk with Jesus.* GTWIs are dangerous because they can stain our reputation as a respectable lady.

Now, I committed all three of these, but I certainly perfected this last one! Whether it was a date leaving my apartment in the early hours of the morning or me departing from his house late at night, I engaged in behaviors that don't look good for a Christian single woman. Moreover, the Word cautions us to not live like the world. More to the point, it's one thing for people to speculate about what we do; it's another to foolishly give them a reason to talk in the first place. We have to be careful that whatever we do doesn't cause us or someone else to stumble into sin. It hurts me to admit that I haven't always followed this line of reasoning. Even beyond dating, I have unwittingly committed GTWIs by spending personal time with friends.

For instance, I enjoy an occasional glass of wine. I never thought about how this type of behavior might make me look to a nonbeliever.

With the reality of Facebook and smartphones with cameras, we believers have to be ever so careful! I can't tell you how many pictures I have foolishly taken with alcohol in my hands. It was not until very recently that I became mindful of how such open behavior could be perceived by the public, thus affecting my witness—no matter how rare it might be. Lord, have mercy! If I could turn back the hands of time! 1 Corinthians 10:32–33 says, "Do not cause anyone to stumble, whether Jews, Greeks or the church of God— even as I try to please everyone in every way. For I am not seeking my own good but the good of many, so that they may be saved."

Now when I want to enjoy a glass of wine, I mainly do it in a private setting, away from the prying eyes of the public. This isn't a hard-and-fast rule, and I don't do it all the time, but I'm trying to be more aware of how my actions can affect others. There will always be those who disapprove of our every movement, no matter

~ Your Reflection Pool ~

how much we try to do right. We can, however, strive daily to live a life that draws nonbelievers to Jesus Christ, not turn them away.

Let's refocus our attention back on marriage. Everyone knows what a wedding is. Even most children can tell you what a bride looks like. But what does it mean to be *"Wedded"*?

According to one definition, to be wedded is *"to marry in a formal ceremony; take as one's husband or wife."* Another meaning is *"to bind by close or lasting ties; to become united or to blend."*

Genesis 2:22–24 gives the best definition: "Then the LORD God made a woman from the rib He had taken out of the man, and He brought her to the man. The man said, 'This is now bone of my bones and flesh of my flesh; she shall be called woman for she was taken out of man. For this reason a man will leave his father and mother and be united to his wife, and they will become one flesh.'"

What did Adam do once God established who his woman was? Did he rush her off to the nearest bush to shack up? No, he did not. He honored Eve in the presence of our Heavenly Father and made a sacred vow to join with her from that day forward.

Let's stay here for a moment. If a man gets hurt, he won't deny himself relief from the pain. If he cannot breathe, he will fight for air. If he's starving, he'll hunt for food.

If he needs a bathroom break, trust me . . . he will take one. He cannot humanly ignore the physical demands of his body. This is why Adam describes Eve as "bone of my bones and flesh of my flesh; she shall be called woman, for she was taken out of man." He is promising his Heavenly Father that she will be as important to him as his own body.

In fact, God's Word in Ephesians 5:28 emphasizes this even more. It says, "In this same way, husbands ought to love their wives as their own bodies. He who loves his wife loves himself." One definition of *marriage* is *"a legally recognized relationship, established by a civil or religious ceremony, between a man and woman who intend to live together as sexual partners."* Stay with me, now! Ephesians 5:23–24 says, "For the husband is the head of the wife as Christ is the head of the church, his body, of which he is the Savior. Now as the church submits to Christ, so also wives should submit to their husbands in everything." The Scripture confirms that *only a wife* should submit everything to her husband. That's why it's so important to have a God-fearing and Spirit-filled husband.

Now the world has deceived us into believing there's an exception to this biblical rule. We are now to believe this sacred order includes any male who calls us Wifey, Boo, Bae, Baby, Baby Mama, partner, girlfriend, lover, mistress, my girl, Shorty, Buddy, whatever. Many unmarried women don't even see themselves as single. They "play wife" to a

❧ Your Reflection Pool ❧

guy who has not honored them as his wife. Don't believe me? Randomly find a large group of women, and ask them to raise their hands if they are single. First, see how many respond. Then go a step further and ask, "How many of you are not married?" Then watch how many raise their hands! Beloved, for the record, *single* by law means *unmarried*.

Essentially, this book is based on two concepts I have coined: *Unwed Wife* and *Unwed Wife Syndrom*e. As such, let's look at what exactly these terms mean and what are the symptoms that identify them.

An *unwed wife* is a *woman who consistently performs the duties of a wife*. Thus, she has set the expectation that she will continue to do so while in a committed relationship with a man who is not her husband. Examples may include cooking for a man on a regular basis, taking care of his sexual needs, shacking and/or creating a family together, playing unmarried stepmom to his biological child(ren), etc.

A *syndrome is a group of things or events that form a recognizable pattern, especially of something undesirable. It might also be called a condition, disorder, or set of symptoms. The Unwed Wife Syndrome is a spiritual virus that blurs one's mindset or perception of how an unmarried daughter of Christ should share her life with a man who is not her husband.* Make no mistake, any woman or young lady can become an unwed wife. You may be a CEO, a pastor's daughter, a doctor, a famous celebrity, a lawyer, a minister's girlfriend, a pageant queen, a principal, a successful entrepreneur—status, age, and profession have little to do with it. Since living as an unwed wife is more common today than ever, I've created the following Code of Conduct that can help anyone stay in the safety zone as a single daughter of Jesus Christ when dating. I truly believe the Holy Spirit guided me in creating this Code, and I encourage you to consider it carefully.

Code of Conduct that Every Daughter of Jesus Christ Should Consider

1. *Do not have sex with a man who is not your husband.*
2. *Do not live with a man who is not your husband unless he is a platonic roommate with whom you have communicated set boundaries in order to avoid a GTWI.*
3. *Do not cook for a man on a* regular *basis who is not your husband.*
4. *Do not perform domestic chores* (cleaning, washing clothes, running errands, babysitting his kids) *on a regular basis for a man who is not your husband.*
5. *Do not create bills with a man who is not your husband or give him free access to your debit and/or credit cards.*
6. *Do not alter or limit your education, career, and/or traveling opportunities in*

life because of a man who is not your husband.

7. *Do not secure a loan, cell phone, or credit card for a man who is not your husband.*
8. *Do not give a man who is not your husband the power to authorize your social calendar.*
9. *Do not give a man unlimited access to your home, car, or life who is not your husband.*
10. *Do not create* (or continue to create) *a family with a man who is not your husband.*

Now, there is one exception. If you and your fiancé are in premarital counseling and your pastor has requested that you disclose certain financial information to one another, by all means do so. I would never suggest marrying anyone without knowing his overall credit and medical history. To do so would be foolish and irresponsible. Nevertheless, we must never justify behaving as a wife before marriage.

If only you knew how ironic it is for me to be writing a book against premarital sex! Years ago, my friend Porscha was the first person I knew who embraced this strange notion called celibacy. None of us within our close knit sista circle were virgins when we married. But here we had one who was talking about no longer wanting to fornicate so she could honor God with the temple of her body before her marriage. We all thought she had lost her mind!

Even to this day, I am ashamed to confess that I ridiculed her decision. "Celibacy . . . that's the most unrealistic thing I've ever heard," I once laughed. "It just gives a man permission to cheat on you! Besides," I argued, "There is no way I'm not testing out my future husband before I get married." Although Porscha and I were both believers, she chose to be obedient to God's Holy Word, which says in 1 Thessalonians 4:3–4 (KJV), "For this is the will

Your Reflection Pool

of God, even your sanctification, that ye should abstain from fornication: that every one of you should know how to possess his vessel in sanctification and honor." All I foolishly cared about, on the other hand, was self. That's why it should come as no surprise to you that I am the one divorced today, and she is still happily married almost twenty years later.

"But" you might say to yourself, *"there is no condemnation in Jesus Christ!"* About which, you would be correct. But we still must ask for forgiveness for our sins. It took me a long time after my divorce to even acknowledge much less confess my sin of shunning my sister's commitment to God. That's why I need you to understand, beloved: regardless of what this modern-day world would have us believe, there are consequences for ignoring the will of God. Please do not choose the same dead-end road I rebelliously took. Remember, the Bible says, "Behold to obey is better than sacrifice" 1

Samuel 15:22 (KJV).

Those words were spoken by the prophet Samuel to Saul, the King of Israel. If obedience was required of an anointed King of Israel, do we really have to wonder whether it's applicable to us? If you are committing fornication like I was, simply repent, ask the Lord to forgive you, and (gasp) *turn away* from it.

Even during the initial writing of this book, I struggled with fornication. Lord knows, I haven't just fallen off the wagon—by the time I came back to my senses, the wagon had traveled onward to another state! If you wonder why I'm being so transparent about my past, it's because I sincerely want you to understand that I'm not here to judge. I have no right to do so. I'm just trying to share with you what I had to learn the hard way. It's not worth falling out of God's grace for a few moments of pleasure. What God has for us is infinitely better in the long term . . . and even in the short term, if the truth be told. Now when I attend a church service or any other event held at the House of the Lord, I can do so with a clear conscience. I no longer bear the secret shame of fornication. Today, I can hold my head up knowing that I am pleasing Christ in this small but significant way. A life that strives to please our Heavenly Father first and foremost is one showered with His peace and blessings.

So, how can we please God through our dating? I'm glad you asked. Ladies, when we get into a dating relationship with a man, we should only reveal a glimpse of what we have to offer as potential wives—as opposed to providing an entire premiere. Now, I'm not saying we shouldn't show our domestic side to the man we love. I've yet to meet a secure man who does not desire his lady to be a gracious hostess. It's great for him to know that we can turn a house into a home without breaking the bank—and let's not underestimate the power of cooking. Today's woman often believes that

❧ Your Reflection Pool ❧

learning how to cook is as prehistoric as the dinosaurs, but she is deluding herself about the seductive power of a tasty homecooked meal. Quite frankly, a delicious dish prepared by the woman he loves is a powerful magnet for most men!

Personally, I am falling back in love with cooking, and *when my future love interest finds me*, I will happily demonstrate some of my favorite meals. I will not, however, allow him to expect them on a regular basis—daily or even weekly—unless he becomes my husband. Notice I said, "when my future love interest finds me," not when I find him. "He who finds a wife finds what is good and receives favor from the Lord" (Proverbs 18:22), not the other way around. Any woman or young lady who truly knows who she is in Jesus Christ should never feel desperate for love. I can say this because it took me forty-seven years before I came to this important realization! Beloved, our Father is the Creator and Commander of the universe. Why should we ever feel like we have to seek out or chase a man? That particular mindset submits to the pressures of the world, not the assurances of the Word of God.

Let's briefly revisit Ephesians 5:24. "Now as the church submits to Christ, so also wives should submit to their husbands in everything." One definition for everything is *all*: a little word with a big meaning. Your genetic "all" is what distinguishes you from other women in the world. We may be short while our neighbor is tall. Our sister may have blonde hair while ours is red. Mom may be fair skinned while her daughter is a beautiful shade of chocolate. We might love structure while our best friend flourishes in cluttered chaos. Whatever the combination of looks, talents, and personal characteristics that define us, the essence of our all or "everything" is only meant to be shared with our spouse.

There are women today who proudly claim the status of *common-law wife*. Please hear me, my sisters: to live a common-law lifestyle is the epitome of being an unwed wife. A c*ommon-law wife* is *"a woman who has lived with a man for years with the 'intent to be married' or performs as a wife although unmarried."* One definition for *common* means *"often occurring or frequently seen;"* another is *"without special privilege, rank, or status."* This particular meaning strikes me most: *without special privilege, rank, or status*. In other words, Beloved, the status of a common-law wife is only for a "common woman." As the daughters of the Most High God, we are anything but common.

In Matthew 12:50, Jesus said, "For whoever does the will of my Father in heaven is my brother and sister and mother." In fact, God's Word tells us that we are to be set apart from the world, not living in a common existence. "But you are a chosen people, a royal priesthood, a holy nation, a people belonging to God, that you may declare the praises of him who called you

Your Reflection Pool

out of darkness into his wonderful light" 1 Peter 2:9. We can only live in "His wonderful light" when our lives reflect His will.

Think about it, my friend. Why in the world would we want to regularly commit to performing as a wife for a man who has not yet earned that right? Won't we have plenty of time to do this once we're married? You could be saying to yourself, "Well, I don't know if I am going to marry him." To which I would respond by asking, "Then why behave as his wife?" That's like decorating a client's home with stunning style and elegance but having her acknowledge someone else for your work. All that work and no proper recognition! That's essentially what happens when we regularly serve the needs of a man who is not our husband. Put in these terms, it's easy to see why the conduct of an unwed wife is so out of order. It simply doesn't make sense. We're working to preserve and build up a mirage.

I cannot tell you how many times I've heard

unmarried or divorced women, some even Christian, profess regarding their relationships, *"I already feel married; all we are missing is a piece of paper!"* It is my fervent belief that we were all created to become wedded wives, either singularly unto the Lord or to Him as well as our husbands.

Now why would I say that? Keep in mind a definition of wedded is "to bind by close or lasting ties; to become united or to blend." When we make God first and foremost in our lives, His will through the Holy Spirit transforms our own, thus binding them together. When our will blends with God's, we unite with Him or become wedded to Him. How can we know when our will is similar to God's? It's quite simple, actually: just obey His holy commandments and His Word. In John 14:21, Jesus tells us, "Whoever has my commands and obeys them, he is the one who loves me. He who loves me will be loved by my Father, and I too will love him and show myself to him."

I often wonder how it makes God feel when we try to manipulate the sanctity of marriage. He purposely created woman to be honored by man. Much like the furnishings leased long-term from rental companies, an unwed wife is on loan. The renter is trying to portray a certain lifestyle that he or she cannot actually afford. The same rule applies to the unwed wife. She is attempting to depict a lifestyle that she does not have, that of a married woman.

In both situations, one option was originally meant to be temporary, while the other is intended to be permanent. That's why it is to our advantage for tax purposes to own a home as opposed to renting one. One option yields benefits, while the other does not. An unwed wife is under a "temporary attachment" by the man she loves, while a married woman is covered under the spiritual covenant of her husband. Thus, the married woman is living according to the will of God. Remember Proverbs 18:22: "He who finds a wife finds what

Your Reflection Pool

is good and receives favor from the Lord." It does not say a live-in girlfriend or life partner; the Word specifies "wife." So when a woman proudly claims that she already "feels married," she is only trying to justify why she is not. My philosophy is that the truth not only hurts, it burns like a hot stove! At least, that's how it has always felt to me. But the truth is, we are living in a world where the things of God are shunned, ridiculed, and compromised, while things opposite to God's Holy Word are gladly embraced and encouraged.

In an article featured in *JET Magazine,* Earl Wright II, a sociologist and associate professor at the University of Cincinnati, claims a number of households headed by single women "a*re destined to struggle in the long-term.*" Dr. Wright also states, *"it's an issue that single women must weigh before they decide to live with—or merely sleep with—men they date. Their choices can lead to a harder life for them and their children."* Truth is many women, whether they have children or not, are seeking love the wrong way like I did. It is up to those of us who have been delivered from our past to serve as a humble voice for all of us. The point of this book is not to rush you into a marriage. It is instead to challenge all of us to think twice before placing ourselves in a situation that could delay or alter our future goals and purpose.

Points to Remember

❒ Those who are controlled by their current circumstances will fail to see the possibilities of what God has in store for their future.

❒ If we trust God for other important aspects of our life (i.e., our healing, a new car or job, etc.), why not trust and wait on Him for our future husband?

❒ Anyone can become an unwed wife. Status, age, and profession have nothing to do with it.

Finished Reading Chapter 1? ***Collect Your 1st Red Diamond.***

Tashma reminds us that, “He who finds a wife finds what is good and receives favor from the Lord,” not *she* who becomes desperate and searches for a husband. In what ways have you perhaps behaved as an unwed wife? How is that affecting your walk with the Lord? What behavioral changes would you like for the Lord to make in you?

2

Whose Daughter Are You Anyway?

"Just like a grain of sand that makes up the ocean shore, we were all created for a purpose."

—Tashma White

Now that we've established *what* an unwed wife is and *who* can become one, let's talk about *why* women become unwed wives in the first place. That day as I was praying in the shower, God revealed to me precisely why I had chosen this way of life. I learned that I was bound by a lifelong struggle with rejection. My father was an alcoholic, and he lost everything because of this disease. As a result, he and my mother divorced when I was young. Although we were close, we never discussed his drinking. When I was eight years old, I decided to write him a letter asking him to stop. I remember sitting at our kitchen table and imprinting my emotions onto some pretty olive-green stationery my mother had given me. When she asked whom I was writing to, I responded, "Daddy about his drinking." She suddenly paused and quietly said, "Baby, sometimes it's hard for the people we love to get the help they need most. It doesn't mean they don't love us, though."

I knew my mother's words were code for "Don't get your hopes up," but I stubbornly ignored her. In my childish mind, Daddy would read my letter, throw away the liquor, and we would be a family again, The End.

Your Reflection Pool

I can't tell you how long it took me to write, erase, and then write again until I was finished with that letter. The day finally came to visit my father for the weekend. Mama came to my room and found me dressed and ready to go. My leg nervously swung up and down as I sat on the edge of my bed patiently waiting. In my left hand was a large brown paper grocery bag, neatly folded at the top, which contained my freshly pressed clothing. The cherished letter was clutched tightly in my right hand. She saw the letter and said, "Oh, little bunny . . . is that your letter?"

"Yes, Ma," I said with a bright smile.

She sadly smiled and said, "Tasha, no matter what happens or doesn't happen, your Daddy does love you."

"I know, Ma, and he's going to stop drinking, too . . . just you wait!"

My father lived with my grandmother, or Mawmaw as we fondly called her. Shortly after arriving at her house, I sought out my dad and told him I had something that I wanted him to read. I tenderly placed the note on the nightstand by his bed, careful not to bend it. Afterward, I went outside with my cousins.

Hours later, I came in the house hot and exhausted from rigorous play. As soon I entered the house, I began to look for my father. I saw Grandma and asked, "Mawmaw, have you seen my Daddy?"

"He just left to go to the store. Go take your bath so that you can get ready for bed," she said.

"Yes, ma'am," I replied and obediently did as I was told. While I was in the bath, I heard Daddy's voice float through the hollow door from the front room. My grandmother said to him disapprovingly, "Moe," as was his nickname, "hide that so she won't see it."

Instantly, I knew what "that" was, and I yelled out from my warm, soapy bathwater, "Daddy . . . did you read my letter?"

After receiving no response, I quickly got out, dried off, and put on my nightclothes. As if the timing were coordinated, his bedroom door shut as soon as I came out of the bathroom. I knocked and tried his doorknob, only to find it was locked. "Daddy, please open up! Did you read it?" I yelled through the door. No sound came from his room, and almost immediately the light went off. I was so disappointed, but I held onto the hope that he just hadn't read my letter yet.

After going to bed that night, I dreamed of how much better our family would be once Daddy came back home. The next morning, I jumped out of bed, dressed, and ran to my father's room. His door was open, and I went inside. The first thing I saw was the crumpled writing paper lying on his nightstand. Numb, I slowly walked over and picked it up. I timidly opened the letter and noticed the writing had become smeared with tearstains. I heard him returning to his room and quickly turned around with my heart in my eyes and the letter in hand. I looked expectantly at him and

❧ Your Reflection Pool ❧

silently pleaded with him to say something.

He never said a word. His only response was to simply turn and walk out of the house. I can't tell you how long I stood there waiting for him to come back. I remember staring off into space as warm, plump tears skied down the sides of my face. Eventually, I came to myself and looked down at the misshapen paper. "All of that hard work . . . for nothing!" I bitterly said out loud.

Suddenly, I tore the note in half, thirds, fourths, and then even smaller pieces. I tore until my hands ached and I could tear no more. With lead feet, I walked to the nearby wastebasket and let the particles fall. Each tiny piece represented an image I had created in my mind for my family's future. I watched with trance-like focus until the last piece of paper settled inside the trash can on top of the other abandoned items that were to be thrown away.

My father and I never stopped loving each other. For what it's worth, he was my daddy, and

I loved him dearly. It was as if we had made an unspoken truce to not discuss the letter, and we never did. In fact, I never spoke of it again to anyone until I was much older and he had passed away. The day that I did, my marriage was long over, and I had begun my plans to move to Texas.

That was the night the Holy Spirit revealed to me that I was bound by the stronghold of rejection. That was why I began each of my relationships by giving more than I ever received emotionally. No matter how badly I was mistreated physically, emotionally, or verbally, even so, I always had the hardest time letting the other person go. In addition, my heart was infested with bitter roots of resentment from my childhood. This contributed to the disintegration of my marriage too. I needed love, but I was fearful of being rejected. So my unspoken motto became to love with a long-handled spoon. I intentionally distanced myself from the warming rays of true companionship.

When I got married, I had not sought the Lord for healing. The remaining pieces of my heart were constantly put on display under a "look but do not touch" glass case. It wasn't until the marriage was done that I drew closer to the Holy Spirit. He slowly began to show me the jagged pieces of my past. The Holy Comforter began pruning and purging my spirit, healing me through the Word of God. I meditated on Scriptures like, "Fear not, for I have redeemed you; I have summoned you by name; you are mine." Isaiah 43:1b Even when I read this today, it soothes the yearning in my soul. It comforts my battered heart to know that the *Great I Am* loves me . . . for me!

The Holy Spirit showed me that there are four primary reasons a woman becomes an unwed wife. The first is a **lack of self-awareness**. A daughter of Christ must know that she is a woman of royal heritage.

To prove my point, let's review one of my favorite love stories in the Bible, that of

❧ Your Reflection Pool ❧

Rebekah and Isaac. In Genesis 24:1–4, their story begins with this description of Isaac's father, Abraham:

> Abraham was now old and well advanced in years, and the LORD had blessed him in every way. He said to the chief servant in his household, the one in charge of all that he had, "Put your hand under my thigh. I want you to swear by the LORD, the God of heaven and the God of earth, that you will not get a wife for my son from the daughters of Canaanites, among whom I am living but will go to my country and my own relatives and get a wife for my son Isaac."

Abraham did not send just any servant, but his most valued one. He knew the significance of choosing the right wife for his son. Canaanites traditionally were idol worshippers, and Abraham knew that this way of life was unacceptable to our Lord God. He did not want a daughter-in-law who would submit to idolatry and who, in turn, could influence his son and grandchildren to do the same thing.

When the servant saw Rebekah filling her jar at the spring, he asked her one of the most important questions ever asked in the Bible: *"Whose daughter are you?"* Genesis 24:47a.

The servant could tell she was a woman of value, because the Word tells us that "without saying a word, the man watched her closely to learn whether or not the LORD had made his journey successful" Genesis 24:21. You see, when a man of God is considering a woman for a wife, he will watch how she carries herself to determine whether or not she has standards. It was clear from Rebekah's demeanor and behavior that she was a woman of God.

Once the chief servant selected Rebekah as Isaac's wife, she prepared to travel to his home. The story continues:

> Then Rebekah and her maids got ready and mounted their camels and went back with the man. So the servant took Rebekah and left. Now Isaac had come from the Beer Lahai Roi, for he was living in the Negev. He went out to the field one evening to meditate, and as he looked up, he saw camels approaching. Rebekah also looked up and saw Isaac. She got down from her camel and asked the servant, "Who is the man in the field coming to meet us?" 'He is my master,' the servant answered. *So she took her veil and covered herself.*" Genesis 24:61–65 (my emphasis)

The Scripture shows that Isaac was a man who spent time with God. It also shows that Rebekah had a strong sense of self-awareness; in other words, she knew who she was. We can tell this because of her actions once she discovers Isaac's true identity. What did she do

Your Reflection Pool

once she realizes he's the wealthy heir she could potentially marry? She *covers herself* to demonstrate that she is a woman of virtue.

This behavior is directly counter to what the world promotes today. Once it's known that a man is privileged and wealthy (an NBA or NFL player, a singer, etc.), the world would have us believe that we should show off our bodies to entice his attention instead of acting like a respectable lady. Rebekah was clearly a lady of quality who respected herself and expected others to respect her. In addition, she didn't think like a man, she *thought like a godly woman*. Most men tend to be hunters by nature. If Rebekah had been thinking like a man, she might have pursued Isaac, not the other way around. But that's not what happened.

Let's move on to Genesis 24:66–67, which says, "Then the servant told Isaac all he had done. Isaac brought her into the tent of his mother Sarah, and he married Rebekah. So she became his wife, and he loved her; and Isaac was comforted after his mother's death."

Notice that Isaac established Rebekah as his wife *before* "he loved her." Once we present ourselves as a virtuous woman, a real man of God will show us a place of honor in his life, not as a form of "Entertainment Tonight."

The second reason women take the status of an unwed wife is a **lack of self-worth.** The love tale in the Bible that most exemplifies what a man will do when he truly loves a woman is the story of Jacob (who was also called Israel) and Rachel. Jacob was one of the twin boys born to Isaac and Rebekah in Genesis 25:21–26. When Jacob grew into manhood and saw Rachel, he instantly fell in love with her. He recognized that Rachel was a woman of quality. Thus, he didn't just approach her like any woman off the street. He did what any real man who respects and honors you will do: he worked to earn her love and affection. Most importantly, he went to her father and asked for permission for her hand in marriage. This brother not only asked for permission, but he *offered* to work seven years for her father to prove he was worthy of her. Genesis 29:9–18

It's important to distinguish a worldly definition of self-worth from a spiritual one. If we're not careful, we can easily drown in the world's version of self-worth. It will have us spending more time on fashion trends than we do training for our jobs. It will help us to justify not paying our tithes. The world teaches us that only those with expensive cars, designer clothes, a home in the Hamptons, and an unlimited supply of VIP tickets are classy and important. But the truth is very different. True class comes from being gracious toward others, regardless of a person's title or socioeconomic background, and from being a hospitable hostess. It comes from honoring other people and maintaining standards of respect for ourselves. Now, don't misunderstand me: I adore nice things and beautiful clothes just like the next woman! I won't, however, allow

~ Your Reflection Pool ~

myself to worship or be defined by them. That's the very meaning of idolatry.

God was serious when He said, "I will have no other gods before Me." Why do you think this is the first commandment? Idols can include material possessions. Our self-worth should not be linked to what we wear or what we own. In fact, the Lord "commands those who are rich in this present world not to be arrogant nor to put their hope in wealth, which is so uncertain, but to put their hope in God, who richly provides us with everything for our enjoyment." 1 Timothy 6:17

God's Word assures us that we are worth much more than material things. Jesus said in Matthew 10:30–31, "And even the very hairs of your head are numbered. So don't be afraid; you are worth more than many sparrows." Psalm 139:13–14 assures us, "For you created my inmost being; you knit me together in my mother's womb. I praise you because I am fearfully and wonderfully made; your works are wonderful, I know that full well." Beloved sister, we are royal heiresses to a kingdom much higher than any man-made thrones!

The third reason women become unwed wives is **lack of self-respect.** Few stories in the Bible demonstrate the value of women as much as the level of respect Boaz had for Ruth. She was a woman of integrity, a widow who honored her mother-in-law, Naomi, through loyalty and lifelong dedication. They only had each other, and as all the men in their immediate family had died, they were extremely poor. One day, Ruth said to Naomi "Let me go to the fields and pick up the leftover grain behind anyone in whose eyes I find favor." Ruth 2:2b

Now, Boaz was a relative on Ruth's deceased husband's side. One day while Ruth was working in his fields, a fateful encounter took place:

Just then Boaz arrived from Bethlehem

> and greeted the harvesters, "The LORD be with you!" "The LORD bless you!" they called back. Boaz asked the foreman of his harvesters, "Whose young woman is that?" The foreman replied, "She is the Moabitess who came back from Moab with Naomi. She said, 'Please let me glean and gather among the sheaves behind the harvesters.'" Ruth 2:4–7

After hearing how hardworking Ruth was, all for the sake of caring for her mother-in-law, Boaz told Ruth:

> "I've been told all about what you have done for your mother-in-law since the death of your husband—how you left your father and mother and your homeland and came to live with a people you did not know before. May the LORD repay you for what you have done. May you be richly rewarded by the LORD, the God of Israel,

Your Reflection Pool

under whose wings you have come to take refuge." Ruth 2:11–12

Boaz continued to watch Ruth (remember what I said earlier: a man who is interested in marriage will watch us to see what values and standards we have). He not only respected her; he also married her! The Lord chose her to be the grandmother of one the greatest figures of the Bible, King David. Ruth carried herself with standards that Boaz recognized as quality.

The fourth and final reason women succumb to the status of being an unwed wife is the **fear of being alone.** Many believe their chances of meeting someone are slim to none. In fact, many women have given up on finding love because it hasn't happened before *their* specific "appointed time."

Ironically, there are slightly more men in the world than there are women. Yes, you read that correctly. According to a recent United Nations report on the world's population, men have a slight lead on the number of women. Males do tend to run the risk of dying earlier than females in their youth and as adults. Nevertheless, there are plenty of men in this world, regardless of where we live. As daughters of the King who created and commands the universe, our potential in all things is limitless, including our love life. That's why we don't have to fall prey to a fear of being alone.

Case in point, I once happened to strike up a random conversation with a woman while standing in line at the Department of Motor Vehicle Registration. I could tell she had something weighing heavily on her mind. So I just listened with a compassionate ear. She shared with me how she was in a toxic relationship and hated it. When I gently asked her, "What's forcing you to stay in it?" she gave me a sad look and said, "I really don't want to be by myself."

Few things can rival the sadness of this

sweet woman's statement. I should know, because I once felt the exact same way. In fact, there are many women (and men) who do. There are even those who feel extreme levels of loneliness. A couple years back, I read about a beautiful young woman who lived outside of Manchester, England, who committed suicide because she was unmarried and childless by the age of thirty. My heart breaks at the weight of hopelessness that she must have felt.

Resources for Those Struggling with Suicide

Emergency Numbers
Suicidestop.com/worldwide_emergency_numbers.html.
This website contains an extensive listing of emergency numbers per country

---

Below are some additional website resources:

Africa
(International Association for Suicide Prevention or IASP)
www.iasp.info

Canada
(Canadian Association for Suicide Prevention)
www.suicideprevention.ca

Spain
(Samaritans in Spain)
www.samaritansinspain.com

UK
England, Ireland, Scotland and Wales
(Samaritans)
www.samaritans.org

United States
(Broken Believers)
www.brokenbelievers.com

If you are secretly struggling with suicidal

urges, please know that God has neither forgotten nor forsaken you, Beloved. If you need to speak with someone, please contact your local emergency services. For more information, please see the sidebar for a listing of resources.

More than anything else, this fear of being alone is why it's so important that we make God our truest source of joy and peace. Deuteronomy 31:6 tells us to "Be strong and courageous. Do not be afraid or terrified . . . for the Lord your God goes with you; He will never leave you or forsake you." Our life has purpose, and we never have to feel lonely regardless of whether we are single or not.

Fear of being alone can have a negative impact not only on you, but on others in your life as well. As single women, we have to be particularly careful that we don't allow ourselves to be vulnerable to men who prey on us. 2 Timothy 3:7 warns, "They are the kind who worm their way into homes and gain control over weak-willed women, who are loaded down with sins and are swayed by all of kinds of evil desires, always learning but never able to acknowledge the truth."

I call this type of men "*grown infants.*" What exactly is a grown infant, you may wonder? *It is an adult individual who never becomes responsible or a productive citizen, thus relying solely upon their mama, daddy, or significant other to provide for them.*

A relationship with a grown infant is built upon what you can provide for him. If you don't work, the bills aren't paid. If you don't pay to renew the inspection sticker on his car, he'll drive with an expired one until he gets a traffic citation. If you don't plan and pay for the vacation, there won't be one. If you don't buy the tickets for the show, then you can't go. In essence, you become his second mother during the day and his lover at night.

Now, to be fair, there are plenty of men who are dealing with female grown infants as well. If it's not fair to us, then it is not fair to our

Your Reflection Pool

brothers in Christ either. No one (regardless if they are a woman or a man) deserves to be shackled to a self-serving person.

Someone once said, "We teach people how to treat us." Beloved, if we want a man to respect us, we must maintain a level of self-respect first. If we want him to be considerate of us, we should never agree to a first date when asked at the last minute. A first date that is proposed at the last minute means he thought of you *last!*

Ladies, we should *never* allow a fear of being alone to force us into becoming a "desperately seeking male" type of woman. Even if we weren't raised with an earthly father to teach us about men and relationships, once we give our life to Jesus Christ, we become a daughter of the Most High God. Deuteronomy 10:17-18a, says, "For the LORD your God is God of gods and LORD of lords, the great God, mighty and awesome, who shows no partiality and accepts no bribes. He defends the cause of the fatherless and the widow."

You may be wondering just how I finally overcame the spirit of loneliness. It is a testimony that I love to share, because it demonstrates just how powerful the Word of God is! In 2013, I became extremely sick and ended up in the emergency room three times within a matter of five days. I couldn't keep anything on my stomach and would wake up out of my sleep gasping for air. It constantly felt like I was choking and couldn't breathe. Turns out I had a severe case of GERD, or Gastroesophageal Reflux Disease, a digestive disorder that affects the lower esophageal sphincter.

Since I live alone, I was terrified of falling asleep at night, which was when I experienced the worse symptoms. My immediate family lived over 900 miles away. In about two and a half months, I lost almost forty pounds. You talk about feeling lonely and forgotten! It was only by God's grace and mercy that I made it through such a dark time. I constantly prayed and spent time studying the Word.

One particular night, the Holy Spirit led me to my all time favorite scripture, Isaiah 41:9–10, which says, "I took you from the ends of earth, from its farthest corners I called you. I said, 'You are my servant'; I have chosen you and have not rejected you. So do not fear, for I am with you, do not be dismayed, for I am your God. I will strengthen you and help you; I will uphold you with my righteous right hand." I meditated on this Scripture daily until I was healed. Before long, the stronghold of loneliness was lifted from me.

The good news, my friend, is that the blessing of this healing applies to you as well. Our Eternal Father doesn't play favorites or honor one of his children above another, so you, too, can receive deliverance from loneliness. That's why you don't have to allow the fear of being alone to bully you.

Your Reflection Pool

Points to Remember

- ❒ An unwed wife has a greater fear of being alone than of Almighty God.
- ❒ As believers, we are royal heiresses to a kingdom much higher than any man-made throne.
- ❒ A *first* date that is proposed at the last minute means he thought of you *last!*

Finished Reading Chapter 2? *Collect Your 2nd Red Diamond.*

Have you allowed a fear of being alone to cause you to settle for an unfulfilling relationship? If so, do you believe this is the relationship that God had originally intended for you? If yes, then why?

3

The Eight Types of Unwed Wife

"A woman's actions usually affect more than her own life."

—Tashma White

As women, I believe we take on the characteristics of an unwed wife long before ever becoming one. Growing up in the small community of Statesville, North Carolina, I was surrouned by unwed wives like an infant in a hospital nursery.

For me, the roots go back more than a generation. My mother neither witnessed regular displays of affection as a child, nor did she ever experience a talk about dating standards with a role model. Furthermore, my grandmother was busy working hard to keep food on the table. Right or wrong, spending quality time with her thin, awkward, and painfully shy teenage daughter was not a priority for her.

Mama's first introduction to her father occurred at age seven, when she and her friends went to buy some treats from the local mom-and-pop shop. She and her buddies ran excitedly toward the olive-colored building, anticipating the taste of their favorite penny candy. Once her little legs reached the graveled parking lot, she noticed a group of men standing near the side of the store. They all stopped and suddenly turned to stare at her. Tall, handsome, and bow-legged, one man in particular stood out. *I've never seen him around here before,* she thought. After

❧ Your Reflection Pool ❧

sparing him a curious glance, she prepared to sprint after her pals who had disappeared through the doors of the store.

"Hey little girl," the stranger called, "come here." She turned and asked, "Who, me?"

"Yeah, come here for a minute," the man said. Having been taught to respect her elders, she didn't see denying his request as an option. She gingerly walked toward the visitor and said, "Yes, sir."

"Do you know who I am?" he asked. "No, sir," she said.

"I'm your daddy," he said in a matter-of-fact tone. A look of astonishment paralyzed the muscles in her face. After a moment of struggle, she shut her mouth, swallowed, and said, *"Oh!"*

He reached inside his pocket, took out a shiny new fifty-cent piece, and said, "Here, go buy yourself some candy."

Mama thanked him kindly and obeyed. Looking back at him over her shoulder, she walked slowly into store. Once inside she quickly snatched up her candy, paid and raced back outside. Her heart pierced with disappointment to find he had gone.

When Mama turned fifteen years old, her mother suddenly died from a heart attack. She and her three younger siblings were then sent to live with my great-grandmother. Although she loved them, she, too, had a hands-off approach when it came to displaying affection. It was a typical textbook case: my mother grew up yearning for acceptance and love. It would be twenty-five years before she saw her father again, and that would be the last time before he died. It wasn't until she became much older that she understood the power of allowing the Lord to heal her from the pain of longing for love.

As a divorcee, I too desire love, but this time around only from my true destined mate. When the Lord blessed me with the revelation of the unwed wife, I revealed it to Mama. Her spirit instantly received it. After explaining the premise of the book, I was astounded to hear her say, "You know, I have been an unwed wife. I was certainly one to your daddy before we married." In an indignant tone, I asked her, "What makes you say that?" I've always been protective of my mom. I won't allow anyone talk negatively about her, not even her own self.

"Tasha, growing up, no one taught me how to date or anything about relationships. I had to learn through trial and sometimes painful error. After your father and I divorced, you know I occasionally dated. Looking back, I'm sure I made mistakes that you saw and followed." Mama went on to say, "I just wish there had been a book like this when I was growing up. God is going to allow you to help a lot of people with it."

I got to thinking about what she'd said. *Goodness, she could be right!* Astonished, I asked myself, *Could living as an unwed wife be a generational curse?* I hadn't considered that.

While I pondered that mind-opener, the

Your Reflection Pool

Holy Spirit whispered the following phrase: "*Do you see what I see*?"

That was my lightbulb moment! I knew then what God was trying to tell me. If we're not careful, we might inadvertently teach our daughters, nieces, sisters, and cousins how to become unwed wives. If a woman has had numerous relationships through the years, guess whose baby girl will most likely become sexually active early? If auntie has shacked with a man, it's usually no surprise when her daughter grows up and does the same thing. If a woman has sex before marriage, take a guess at whose little sister will likely follow her example.

I want to be careful to note that no one is coerced into following another's example. You aren't fated to make mistakes just because your family did! Just because a loved one makes a choice that changes their life doesn't mean we have to do the same. But to believe that those that grow up around us will never mimic our lifestyle and behaviors can only be described in one word . . . *naive!*

Now, before you fall out with me and blow me up on Twitter, let's pause here for a full minute. Please hear what I am trying to say. I didn't write this book to offend you or anyone else. But with love I must be truthful, even when that truth is directed at me as well. The majority of us do have a choice in the decisions we make, and one of the biggest is deciding whether to behave as someone's unwed wife. Our choice affects us and others. It's long past time we took responsibility for our own decisions in this area.

I do want to be careful to point out that not everyone has a choice. A victim of sexual abuse or human trafficking does not have a choice in the crimes committed against her, and most importantly, she does not deserve it—not ever. For women in these situations, the decision to perform as an unwed wife is forced upon them. To be clear, this book is only referring to unwed wives with a choice, not innocent victims.

There are so many things out of order in today's world, and unfortunately, we've simply grown accustomed to them. That's why a great number of Christians thirst more for the advice of their favorite entertainers than they do for the Word of God. Some of these same celebrities treat marriage like an unattainable illusion, like catching a cloud in a jar. If they say, "No marriage for me," then sadly, that's all it takes for some of us to follow their lead. Quite frankly, I used to be just as guilty as they are, maybe even worse. Even still, once we know better, our Eternal Father requires us to do better.

1 Timothy 4:1–2 warns, "The Spirit clearly says that in later times some will abandon the faith and follow deceiving spirits and things taught by demons. Such teachings come through hypocritical liars, whose consciences have been seared as with a hot iron." As believers of Jesus Christ, we should be careful of any advice that

Your Reflection Pool

is counter to the Holy Word. If you are struggling with what you've just read, that's fine. Please just ask yourself, "Who do I care most about? Is it a man-made idol (that celebrity) or the only One who can save me and grant me entrance into heaven?"

Truth is, if we want to date without a life of regret, we must wait on and trust the Creator of All Things. You have no idea how long it took me to finally accept this! But when we fail to do so, we can fall prey to becoming one of the many types of unwed wives.

I've witnessed every classic case in my journey to adulthood. As a result, I've narrowed unwed wives down to eight different types—many of which I have personally been at one point or another!

The Eight Types of Unwed Wife Are as Follows:

The "I Can't Make It By Myself" Unwed Wife

This is the woman who believes she can't pay her bills, get a house, or survive financially on her own. While most women strive to make their own path, this woman is full of excuses as to why she cannot. Her motto is, *"I need a man to save me!"* Forget the fact that she was surviving long before she met that man. In most cases, there are children involved, who may not necessarily be his. She's easily overwhelmed at the perceived pressure of finding other resources to make up for the financial gap should the man leave. The thought of trusting God instead of that man is something she won't even allow herself to consider. The Word of God warns us in Isaiah 2:22 "Stop trusting in man, who has but a breath in his nostrils. Of what account is he?"

The "I'm Going to Fix Him" Unwed Wife

Often this sister has had everyone from his friends to his own mother tell her that he's not good for her. With so many against him, she convinces herself that they (those who have known him all his life) must be proven wrong! The reality is she's the one who comes up short in the end. She won't even realize until it's too late that she's on the same side of the field as all the other people he's used throughout his life. We can't change that man, ladies. Only our Lord God can change him! 2 Corinthians 5:17 says, "Therefore, if anyone is in Christ, he is a new creation; the old has gone, the new has come!"

The "I Need Love" Unwed Wife

This is the classic category my mother fell under. She wasn't raised with love and affection. As a result, she found someone she hoped would give her that. Many women find themselves here. Sometimes, the first man who claims to love these gentle spirits can be the one who ends up hurting them the most. The Word reminds us of God's love for us. Take heart, sweet sister! The Lord of lords and the King of kings loves YOU eternally! Romans 5:8

❧ Your Reflection Pool ❧

(NASB) says, "But God demonstrates His own love toward us, in that while we were yet sinners, Christ died for us."

The "I Got to Have Him" Unwed Wife

This lady will defy her own parents in order to have a particular man. In most cases, she's been raised to have what she wants, and if that man is what's next, then so be it. The problem that usually occurs for this unwed wife is that she's typically the one left holding the bag. This is, of course, after that man she so proudly turned her back on everyone for ends up leaving or hurting her anyway. Take a guess at what happens when we refuse to let go of that man whom everyone has warned us against? "Do not be misled: 'Bad company corrupts good character.'" 1 Corinthians 15:33

The "I Can't Believe He Chose Me" Unwed Wife

This woman's man is most often as smooth

as satin and handsome as sin . . . at least in her eyes! She'd cut you with a butter knife if you didn't agree that he is every woman's dream. No matter what he does, her mission in life is to keep him by any means necessary. The sad part is that it usually takes the best years of her life to realize one woman can't keep him anyway—or rather, that most have already had him. Don't you know that God loves you so much that "Indeed, the very hairs of your head are numbered. Don't be afraid; you are worth more than many sparrows." Luke 12:7

The "He Loves Me, He Loves Me Not" Unwed Wife

I have personal experience with this one. An old flame whom I loved deeply always told me he loved me, but he never showed it when it mattered most. I allowed him to place me on a permanent yo-yo. He only mustered up interest in me when he perceived someone else holding my attention. I've since learned that we teach people how to treat us. I no longer allow myself to be used as any man's sidepiece. God's love for us is always sincere. Ephesians 2:22: "And in him you too are being built together to become a dwelling in which God lives by his Spirit."

The "A Piece of Man Is Better Than No Man at All" Unwed Wife

This beloved daughter suffers from a lack of self-love and self-respect. She's felt this way for so long that she believes any man in her life is better than none at all. Ultimately, she believes that if he goes, she might not have a chance of ever finding anyone else. It's hard for her to grasp the fact that there are over 3 billion men in this world. Most importantly, if she patiently waits on God, she'll be able to drop that piece in order to find her God-given whole. "A (wo)man of many companions may come to ruin, but there is a friend who sticks closer than a brother." Proverbs 18:24.

Your Reflection Pool

The "I'm in Denial" Unwed Wife

She is the most dangerous of all eight types of unwed wives. Why, you might ask? This is the unwed wife who will justify shacking or sleeping with her man until the day she dies. In her mind, her situation is different from all the other unwed wives. She's wears the "we don't need a piece of paper to feel married" badge with honor. Unfortunately, her version of marriage and God's version don't line up. I can promise you, anything that God declares is not up for human debate! Remember, beloved sister, the Holy Creator will never adjust His standards for our lifestyle, nor should He. "Every word of God is flawless; he is a shield to those who take refuge in him. Do not add to his words, or he will rebuke you and prove you a liar." Proverbs 30:5–6.

Points to Remember

❒ Living as an unwed wife can be a generational curse of learned behavior

❒ There are eight types of unwed wives. Not one of these lifestyles benefits an obedient daughter of Christ.

Finished Reading Chapter 3? *Collect Your 3rd Red Diamond.*

Which type of Unwed Wife do you relate to most and why? Today's behavior does not have to keep us in bondage in our future; the difference is a choice!

4

The Enemy in the Mirror

"The fact is, the only person we will ever really know is our self*—and even she changes from time to time."*

—Tashma White

Many parents today inadvertently encourage their daughters to become unwed wives. How so, you may ask? By persuading them to settle on their first serious boyfriend straight out of high school or college. They might miss the importance of taking the time to discover who they are first and what they may truly want out of life later. I would venture to say that we all need access to wise counsel, no matter what age we are, and no one is wiser than the Holy Spirit. It is He who can prevent us from becoming our own worst enemy.

An *enemy*, according to the dictionary, is *"someone whose aim is to sabotage your future goals and inspirations; a person who does not have your best interest at heart; a person whose influence will damage your integrity and reputation."* If we're not careful, an enemy in the mirror can emerge from within us. Growing up, most of us had to live under the house rules set by our parents or guardians for the first stages of our life. Why then should we rush into a serious commitment by living with a man right after high school or college? You have not given yourself a chance to experience the freedom of becoming your own woman.

Surviving on your own separates the real women from the underdeveloped mindset of young girls. If you're under the illusion that you cannot survive out there in the world unless your boyfriend or baby daddy pays your bills, you do yourself a grave injustice! What exactly do you think you were doing before you met that man? Okay, maybe your mom, dad, aunt, uncle, grandma, or grandpa did support you. My question is, so what? There's nothing wrong with working two jobs to make ends meet, and you *can* do it.

When I first went to college, I worked as a dishwasher at two of the local restaurants on campus. One shift started at 6 AM, while the second began at 1:30 PM. I have even cleaned houses to make extra cash. Many of my previous jobs were less than glamorous. However, they allowed me to grow in grace and appreciation for God's blessings. Although I was nowhere near saved during those days, I did know that with God . . . all things are possible!

Your Reflection Pool

Don't be your own enemy by denying yourself an opportunity for self-development. Take time to discover who you first before prematurely deciding to settle down.

Now, here's something to consider for my lovely sistas who, like me, passed the threshold of womanhood some time ago. I don't personally have children of my own, but I know many phenomenal women who've worked extremely hard to raise their children as a single parent. Furthermore, they've molded them to be independent and productive citizens. Imagine those same incredible women getting tangled up with a man who requires more work than their very own children or grandchildren.

Envision a single mother who has been tied down raising her kids for the past eighteen years or so, and now they're graduated and moving on. Finally! She has the freedom to travel and spend her hard-earned money on herself for the first time in a long while. But instead of trusting God, whom she leaned on to help raise her kids, she would rather trust that girlfriend (who isn't even in a healthy relationship herself) to direct her on where to find love. She allows loneliness to be her constant companion, and he has persuaded her not to be so "picky" when it comes to men because of her age. This is how an established woman adorns herself with the fragrance of desperation. In the blink of an eye, she can easily find herself involved with a man who was never meant to be in her life in the first place. Her previously vivacious and peaceful life is now dogged by constant stress and nonstop drama. All of which can be avoided when we let God, not ourselves, choose our future mate.

When we find ourselves in such a situation, we can't place the blame on anyone else. If we've allowed our goals and aspirations to be hindered, we should point the blame at the person solely responsible for our choices—the enemy staring back at us in the mirror. When we get real about our own responsibility, we can start to make new choices.

Making the wrong assumptions when dating can also sabotage us in a major way. Few things can lead us down the road of regret faster than presuming the wrong thing, particularly when dating. If you love hard like I do, it's easy to deny the obvious and instead create in your mind the idea of a love that does not actually exist.

I've listed nine dangerous assumptions below that you never want to make when dating. They are blindfolds of denial that we consciously wear only when we want to avoid the reality of our situation. If any of these sound familiar to you, you're not alone. I too previously believed all of these at some point.

So What If He's Not Saved? That Won't Affect Me

I'll be the first to admit that it's emotionally turbulent to meet a man that we are really attracted to, only to be disappointed in

❧ Your Reflection Pool ❧

discovering that we would be unequally yoked with him. Many women have the strength to move on with their life. Unfortunately, some will do what I did in the past and make excuses to hold onto him anyway. I've since learned the hard way that nothing in this world is more important than our relationship with God, and I do mean nothing! Hence, when we choose to ignore God's Word to follow our own way of doing things, it will affect us negatively, whether we want to admit it or not. The point is, how can we willingly submit our life to a man who does not acknowledge our God? Trust me, I didn't always ask myself these hard questions either. Now, I know better!

In today's world, if that fabulous guy has wealth, success, or a face and body that render us speechless, many would advise us to go for it! Those same misguided individuals would say, "So what if he's not saved. *You* might just be the one to help bring him to Christ." This is what drives many of us to use our hearts as bait and go fishing in the polluted waters of compromise, just to get any bite of male interest. Once we do, it's easy to become blind through the thrill of the catch. So much so, that we don't realize we've caught a spiritual piranha until we've taken it home and tried to make it a part of our life.

The truth is, sweet sister, we can love whomever we want. We should remember, though, that the Lord never gave us permission to settle for an unsaved mate. Furthermore, His Word will never support us marrying a man who refuses to believe in Him. 2 Corinthians 6:14 (KJV) says, "Be ye not unequally yoked together with unbelievers." Why should this even matter? Being bonded with someone who does not share our core Christian values could influence us to become weak in our own spiritual walk.

Abraham understood this better than most, which is why he did not want his son Isaac to wed just anyone. Fast-forward to today, and not much has changed. Yes, my beloved sister, you might influence him into getting saved. But are you willing to give up years of your life until this *might* possibly happen? When we look at it like this, why should any of us settle for such uncertainty? Instead of that man drawing closer to the Lord, he might influence you to pull away from Him. That's why the dating myth, *"So, what if he's not saved, that won't affect me"* is false. It will not only affect you, sweet love, it could spiritually corrupt you as well.

I Know He Cares, Because He's Jealous of Me

Most of us can probably remember at least one toy from our youth that didn't hold much interest for us—until our sibling, cousin, or friend wanted to play with it. That was when that otherwise forgotten item instantly became the object of our affection. This type of behavior is typical of the *"I don't want it, but I don't want anyone else to have it either"* thought process. This mindset is often the nucleus of a jealous

Your Reflection Pool

spirit.

As painful as it is for us to admit, sometimes a man's jealousy has more to do with selfishness than real love. Instead of a toy, the object in question is you! The cliché now reads, *"I don't want you, but I don't want anyone else to have you either."* The reality is, we women are emotional and verbal creatures, whereas men are usually the complete opposite. They will most likely show their genuine feelings through actions. (In the same regard, the same rules apply to us women as well. Many of us don't become jealous of that nice guy we previously shunned until someone else shows an interest in him. In which case, we are just as wrong.)

All in all, sweet sister, the myth that *"I know he cares for me because he's so jealous of me"* is false. Jealousy *does not always* mean he really loves us. Sometimes, it simply means he's selfish.

If I Don't Have Sex with Him, I'll Lose Him

The sad news is, no one believes this myth more than women. We are usually the first to teach that daughter, friend, niece, or sister that if she does not have sex with the man she loves, she will lose him. Oftentimes, instead of encouraging others to honor Christ through celibacy, we inadvertently support that man's case, which is simply that he cannot survive without sex.

Interestingly enough, the criticism I have encountered for my choice to live a celibate lifestyle as a single woman comes mostly from women who had sex before marriage. Some have tried to make me feel as if my decision is the craziest thing in the world. One woman once rudely asked, "Why celibacy? People are going to probably think you're a lesbo!" My response was, "Since I'm not a lesbian, I couldn't care less what ignorant people think."

Never, and I do mean *never*, has this lifestyle choice of mine been questioned or mocked by women who remained virgins until marriage. They understand my commitment to now live a life that honors God—and they don't have regrets about their past choices.

You see, we women don't always realize that if we lose that man because of our celibacy, then he was never worth our time in the first place. Beloved, should you refuse to have or discontinue to have sex with the man you love, I cannot honestly promise that he will not find someone else to satisfy his needs. What I can promise, however, is that we serve a God with whom the word *impossible* does not apply. Don't believe me? Show me in the Bible where the Lord declares something is impossible for Him to achieve. (Save yourself the trouble, sweet sister . . . you *won't* find it!)

What you will find instead is Matthew 19:26, which reads, "What is impossible with man is possible with God." If that brother claims he has to move on because he can't survive without sex, *let . . . him . . . go!* I know

Your Reflection Pool

better than anyone that yes, it will hurt for a while. You might cry many nights from the pain and loneliness. But you will, *if* you give yourself enough time, survive! Want to know how I know? What did you do before you met him? *You were surviving!* Didn't you wake up every morning before you met him? *Yes, you survived!* Weren't you alive and well before you met him? *Yes, you survived!* Hadn't you discovered laughter long before you ever laid eyes on him? *Yes, you survived!* Then trust me when I say, you can also survive if he leaves over your choice to honor God.

As you grow stronger over time, rest in the knowledge that we serve a God who specializes in the unimaginable. He will turn that heartache into joy by sending you the man who is truly worthy of your love and total devotion. As a result, the belief that *"If I don't have sex with him, I'll lose him"* is not always true. And if you *do* lose him, he wasn't worthy of your time in the first place!

I No Longer Need My Girlfriends Now That I Have a Man

First of all, few things in life are more dangerous than making a mere mortal your only source of happiness. Sure, we do that with Jesus —but He's our way to eternity! And yes, many people in our lives should be honored, loved, and appreciated. Many should be commended for their godly character and good deeds. But it doesn't matter how many Tony, Stellar Awards, Grammys, Oscars, or millions someone may have! It doesn't matter how large a pastor's congregation is, how massive a celebrity's fan base, or even the number of letters that follow a name—*only* God deserves to be worshipped! Not only did Jesus unselfishly die for us, He's always there when we need Him most.

Second, as important as romance feels, it's equally important that we remember others who have been there during the most significant moments of our life. Think of your best friend.

She was there when your heart was broken. It was she who gave you never-ending support when you were blindsided by trials and tragedy. She helped fill your lonely hours on New Year's Eve and Valentine's Day. It was she who provided a way for you to go on that cruise when you couldn't afford it. And she's still the one who never forgets your birthday. And yet, when some of us meet a man who appears to be our lifelong dream come true, we often choose to forget that sister who was there first.

Sure, a relationship built on the bond between two friends is completely different than the love shared between a man and woman. However, both should be treasured and respected. If that beloved sista girl was a blessing when you were single, why has she now become an afterthought simply because you are now in a romantic relationship?

Few things in life are sillier than putting a person on a pedestal. Just remember that a pedestal's circumference is very small. It is

Your Reflection Pool

designed to support a person's bottom, not his or her entire body. Hence, the reason they eventually fall off anyway! If you have valuable friends, don't throw away gems that will increase in value over time! You know when someone is a negative weight around your neck versus a soothing beam of light. One will cause you to sink amidst the waves of tribulation, while the other will guide you back to the safety of shore.

If you are dealing with jealous friends, that's a different issue—your friends should want your happiness just as much as you do. So if a friend is behaving in a selfish and jealous manner, then it is she who is wrong. But if your best friends have been a blessing throughout the years, don't allow the attention of a man to extinguish the radiance of your unique friendship. Or else, when the day does come and your man-made god falls off his pedestal, it may be you who finds yourself all alone with only the shattered pieces of that idol left to comfort you.

Even if the romance is solid, fulfilling and godly, maintaining a relationship with friends who are a positive influence in our life is extremely beneficial. Furthermore, they can share a gift that no man can ever offer: the understanding and support of knowing what it's like to be a woman in love. This is why the statement that *"I no longer need my girlfriends now that I have a man"* is false. In order to maintain a healthy balance in our personal life, we not only need the love of a great man, but also the blessing of close friends.

He'll Change for the Better Once We're Married

For single women, refusal to face the truth can sometimes not only be dangerous but deadly. Denial makes it easy for us to ignore obvious signs of disrespect or even worse, indifference when we are lonely and desperate for companionship. When we are in this particular mindset, we can easily overlook behavior that would make us furious were it done to our best friend.

Be careful to watch how he handles you, especially in public. Let me tell you, beloved, there are many things that can hurt you. However, few rival a man who will talk to you rudely in front of your family and friends. You see, we not only teach folks how to treat us, but they also teach us what we can expect from them. If he doesn't call when he says he will, keep it moving. If he can't be around crowds and tries to ruin the mood when you're with your family or friends, run the opposite way. If you have to pay in order for him to take you on a date, my beautiful sister . . . do yourself a favor and terminate that association! Has he ignored your call in an emergency? If so, *please* save yourself a bucket of tears and the future expense of a divorce attorney. It is not worth it! The assumption that *"he will change for the better once we're married"* is false. The only person who will change is *you!* There are

❧ Your Reflection Pool ❧

billions of respectful and considerate men in this world, my sibling in Christ. Diligently seek the Lord and ask Him to bring you the right one.

If He's Good to His Mom, He'll Be Good to Me

Ever since I was a little girl, I've been told that if a man is good to his mama, he will be good to his wife. Never has a bigger lie been told! There are countless stories of men who worship the ground their mothers walk on but verbally and physically abuse their women. To be fair, the same could be said for some women. Many see their fathers through the eyes of hero worship but never give their own husbands or significant others the same level of consideration. This is equally wrong!

Nevertheless, my spiritual sibling, we should never assume because a man is good to his mom, sister, aunt, or grandmother, that he will also be good to us. I was once in a relationship with a man who treated his mother like she was porcelain china. Sadly, that same level of respect did not apply to me. Case in point: one night after we had a small argument, he suddenly snatched open the shower door while I was standing with my eyes closed under a soothing, steady stream of hot water trying to calm down. Before I could do anything more than blink a few times, he threw a large glass of cold water on me. He then proceeded to spit *(yes . . . you read that correctly . . . spit)* in my face! Again, that was behavior that I allowed from a man who treated his mother like fine gold.

Things didn't get better until I put my big girl boots on, decided enough was enough, and left for good. The assumption that *"if a man is good to his mom, then he'll be good to me"* is false. Dear heart, don't base a man's potential on how he treats his mother. Instead, pay attention to how closely he walks with Christ. If the Lord is truly directing his steps, he won't only adore his mother, he'll cherish you as well.

He Doesn't Mean What He Says

One of the things I find most attractive in a man is when he says what he means and means what he says. I would rather have the truth any day of the week. Thankfully, I have found that most men are this way. No, I mean it . . . seriously! We women can't always point the finger, you know. We have a few members on our team who don't always tell the truth either, now (lots of love). Okay, so back to my point.

If he says, *"I don't like you in that dress,"* then trust that he really doesn't. If he tells you, *"I wish you would fix yourself up more,"* don't ignore that. He's being real. When he casually mentions that he likes your hair longer, he has no reason to lie.

Now, there's nothing wrong with being truthful. But can he be truthful without being rude or hateful? That is the question! It goes without saying that if he is a liar, that's a whole other can of *"what a mess!"* It's not worth being in a relationship with someone you can't trust.

Your Reflection Pool

Either way, my sister, don't have your spirit broken by someone who doesn't treasure you. On the other hand, we must make sure we do not ruin our future relationships by being overly sensitive. No one should have to walk on eggshells when they are around us. It is a healthy mind and spirit that can receive constructive criticism both personally and professionally.

The assumption that *"he doesn't mean what he says*" is false. Most men do tend to mean what they say. We just need to have unfiltered ears to listen.

If I Have His Baby, Then I'll Have Him

The words that stand out to me most from this assumption are *if* and *then.* When we operate under this way of thinking, we create a chain of reactions that seldom works in our favor. The only trap set is the one we set for ourselves. Just because a boy or man enjoys having sex with us doesn't mean he loves us.

Any intentional plan to get pregnant in the hopes of holding onto him is wrong and delusional.

The only victim in this scenario is the blameless child, who doesn't ask to be here in the first place. I can't tell you how many embittered baby mamas I've met who lack the discipline not to bad-mouth their baby daddy around the child he fathered, particularly when he moves on with his life with another woman —but they rarely acknowledge their own role in the matter. All of this is difficult for a child. Friend, no one deserves a prison of drama, particularly not an innocent daughter or son. *The belief that "If I have his baby, then I'll have him" is false*. The only way a man will choose to be in our life is if he wants to, not because we force him. Lifelong commitment grows from the seeds of a willing and honest choice, not from those planted by deceit and manipulation.

We've Been Together So Long, I Know He's Going to Marry Me

Dearest, just because a man gives us years of companionship does not mean he wants to marry us. You'd be surprised how many couples stay together out of convenience, not love. Time and time again, I have seen both women and men sacrifice their potential future simply to stay with someone who is *familiar*. No, not because he or she is romantic, considerate, respectful, dependable, or trustworthy but . . . *familiar*.

To make matters worse, family and friends may enable this mindset by constantly reminding the couple, "You all have been together for so long, why not get married?" Oh, how I cringe when I hear these words! The reality is, the only man who deserves our unwavering devotion is our husband, not a play hubby. It's unfortunate to see a woman willingly place her life on hold based on the assumption of an upcoming marriage proposal.

❧ Your Reflection Pool ❧

I was watching a television show the other day where a couple was getting married. The groom-to-be told his girlfriend after they had dated for three years, "If we're together for another ten years, then I'll marry you." Apparently, she chose to give up ten more years of her life and wait for him to make his decision. After their thirteenth anniversary, he finally decided to marry her. Now, while she dutifully waited all those years, that didn't stop him from getting her pregnant with twins. No, it just kept him from honoring her before God and family.

To be fair, I've seen good men do this for a woman as well. Happiness in love should not be exclusive to only women. For the record, our brothers in Christ are equally as deserving!

My sista, we were meant for much more than the waiting game. *The waiting game is a mind game we women choose to play with ourselves in the grand hopes that a particular man will eventually decide to settle down and marry us*. As life moves on, we lose the best years of our youth . . . *waiting* . . . asking . . . fussing . . . threatening . . . hoping . . . *waiting!*

Dearest, we truly deserve better. Think of it like this. When the Lord created you in your mother's womb, He didn't say, "My purpose in creating (insert your name) is that someday she will fall madly in love with a man who refuses to see that she is worthy of honor." Sounds ridiculous, doesn't it? No father wants a man to take advantage of his adored daughter. *Why should our Heavenly Father feel any differently?* Proverbs 11:16 says, "A gracious woman attains honor." *Honor is defined as a place of distinction, recognition, and privilege.* God wants us to have a place of honor or distinction in our relationship with the man we love.

Even a man trying to establish his career can still propose marriage along with an engagement ring. Now, he may not be able to afford the one you have your heart set on at that time. Nevertheless, you should appreciate the fact that he has honorable intentions. (Besides, he can always upgrade your ring during one of your anniversaries.)

The fact is, I have seen a lot of intelligent women fall for an *E-WAR Hustle. E-WAR stands for "Engaged Without A Ring." A "hustle" is "a fraud or swindle." This type of engagement is typically based on fraud. It's a commitment with no tangible evidence that the engagement actually exists.* Now, before you send me an angry email or tweet, please hear me out! I understand it's not the ring that keeps a couple together; it's the commitment that two people choose to keep. Nevertheless, the ring is essential. It publicly symbolizes the eternal devotion that a man gives to one specific woman. It tells the world he has chosen her from among all women. An engagement ring indicates reverence for a man's future bride—to her and to both their families.

All in all, when we wait years for a man to

Your Reflection Pool

marry us, we run the chances of foregoing the respect that we deserve. Like I said before, it's one thing to wait for your careers to become established. It's another to hang on for years while he drags his feet.

A stand-up type of guy won't refuse to respect us if we require it. It's better to walk away heartbroken with your dignity still intact than to stay only to realize he never wanted to marry you in the first place. That's why the assumption, *"We've been together for years, so I know he's going to marry me"* is false. If a man is sent to us by God, the only hustle we will encounter is the one performed on the dance floor, not the one intentionally used to play games with our heart.

10 Thought-Provoking Questions to Consider Before Entering into a Relationship

1. Does his actions say he has fully surrendered his life to the Lord and

Savior, Jesus Christ? (Not simply going to church on Sundays—is his *whole life* lived to honor God?)

2. Does he act and speak respectfully toward you?
3. Does he tithe?
4. Can you trust him to be financially responsible (paying bills on his own)?
5. Can you depend on him when you need him most?
6. Does he make you feel like you have to change in order to be with him?
7. Is he as exclusive with you as you are with him?
8. Does he always take the side of his kids or family over you?
9. Is he abusive, verbally or physically?
10. Does he respect your time alone with your friends?

I wish someone had sat me down in my youth and made me consider some of the things on this list. They may appear petty until you look up and realize you're in love with a living nightmare. For instance, let's look at question 1: *"Do his actions say he has fully surrendered his life to the Lord and Savior, Jesus Christ?"*

If we are Christians, should we really care if the guy we're dating is a Christian too? The world tells us that opposites attract—but the Bible admonishes us in 2 Corinthians 6:14, "Do not be yoked together with unbelievers." Furthermore, 2 Corinthians 6:17 says, "Therefore come out from them and be separate, says the Lord." The truth is, anyone who rejects the teachings of Jesus Christ could potentially influence us to sway in our own beliefs. If you're already married and your spouse is unsaved, that's one thing. You have to find a way to make it work. But if we are saved and choose to date a person who is unsaved, that's something entirely different! The Lord does not want us to compromise our salvation for anyone, especially for someone who is not

~ Your Reflection Pool ~

our spouse.

Now consider question 3, *"Does he tithe?"* Why should this matter, you ask? Malachi 3:8–9 reads:

> "Will a man rob God? Yet you rob me. But you ask, 'How do we rob you?' In tithes and offerings. You are under a curse—the whole nation of you because you are robbing me."

How can a Christian man be head of his household and yet not honor God's Word on tithing? It is his job to cover the spiritual and physical well-being of his family. In addition, he should lead by example, not just by giving commands. This is why as daughters of Christ, we have to be so careful of who we allow into our atmosphere. I cannot say it enough: just because a man goes to church on Sunday does not make him godly. The same, of course, applies to us women! When we don't tithe, we invite curses over our finances, indeed our entire lifestyle. It is a blatant form of distrust toward our Lord and Savior.

Avoiding a Lifetime of Regret

Now that we've looked at some dangerous assumptions that we woman can make when dating, let's shift our energy back to the topic at hand, the enemy in the mirror. When a woman falls in love with a man, there's something that he possesses that draws her to him. Forget what anyone else thinks . . . we know what we like! This is why the honeymoon period of a new relationship is so special for us. We can find everything to smile about during that "new love" phase. Unfortunately, when that male was never designated by God to be in our lives in the first place, that phase tends to wear off like the new car scent in a vehicle. Even when the hazard signs begin to flash, some of us will do what I did and ignore them.

This is why it's important that we get real

about our assumptions, blind spots, and choices. How many of us thought the first guy we had sex with would be our one and only? How many teen mothers assumed they would never get pregnant? How many women over the age of fifty are now infected with HIV/AIDS because they assumed it was a disease for younger women? How many young girls who have contracted an incurable disease ever thought something like that would happen to them? One moment of passion, and now they are suffering with a lifetime of medical tests, painful symptoms, and mandatory prescription drugs.

No one deserves to be judged for a disease that many of us would have were it not for God's grace and mercy. Only hypocrites throw stones when they themselves have lived in glass houses. I confess I have not lived anything near a perfect existence. Nevertheless, I am now allowing the Holy Spirit to deliver me from being my very own enemy in the mirror. I've grown weary of living life with the same

☙ Your Reflection Pool ☙

approach but expecting a different result. That only limits, and possibly destroys, our God-given purpose.

Speaking of our purpose, for a moment, create an image of people suddenly being able to fly. Filled with astonishment, your eyes follow the zooming patterns as they soar effortlessly above you in the sky. Excitedly, you will your body to lift up into the atmosphere so you can experience the same miracle. But to your horror, nothing happens—you remain firmly planted on the ground. Looking down, you see your feet are bound in chains. You cry out in despair, "Lord, why are my feet chained to the ground while everyone else is allowed to fly?"

Suddenly the Lord responds, "My precious daughter, the only one who has ever held you captive . . . *is you*."

Jeremiah 29:11 tells us, "'For I know the plans I have for you,' declares the LORD, 'plans to prosper you and not to harm you, plans to give you hope and a future.'" God promises to open doors of opportunities created specifically for us. The problem is no one knows how long He will choose to keep them open. Sadly, many people will fail to fulfill their purpose in life due to sin. I can assure you that I can't judge anyone. Fact is, I almost missed out on fulfilling my God-ordained purpose to complete this book due to my previous sin. Only by His grace and mercy was I able to finish it, and you, praise God, are able to read it now!

Colossians 1:11–13 reminds us that we are "being strengthened with all power according to his glorious might so that you may have great endurance and patience, and joyfully giving thanks to the Father, who has qualified you to share in the inheritance of the saints in the kingdom of light." Isn't it a blessing to know that no matter what we've done and who we've done it with, if we repent and turn away from sin, God will forgive us!

He reminds us in Isaiah 43:1b: "Fear not, I

have redeemed you; I have summoned you by name." No matter what names we've been called in the past, my friend, our birth name is royal and precious in the sight of our Lord!

Points to Remember

- ❒ Are you inadvertently encouraging other women or girls in your life to become unwed wives? If so, in what way are you doing this?
- ❒ Making the wrong assumptions when dating not only sabotages our future but also our purpose.
- ❒ The Lord has significant plans for your future. The only one who can keep you from them is . . . *you!*

Finished Reading Chapter 4? *Collect Your 4th Red Diamond.*

Asking ourselves the right thought-provoking questions can save us from a life of disappointing relationships. Which three questions listed in chapter 4 do you wish you had asked before beginning your last relationship?

5

The Five Main Ingredients to a Woman's Love Life

"The main ingredient to a successful life is obedience to God."

—Tashma White

What do basic chicken salad and relationships

have in common? They both consist of five main ingredients. A simple chicken salad recipe consists of chicken, celery, mayonnaise, onion, and seasoning. Now granted, depending on what I'm in the mood for I may throw in herbs, spices, chopped pecans, cranberries, or grapes to liven up the taste—but there are only five bare basic ingredients. (I did tell you I love to cook, right?) Similarly, there are five main factors that affect a woman's life when in a relationship. They are *time, home, money, sex,* and *gifts*.

Notice *time* is listed first. Why, you may ask? Time is our most precious resource. It is the one thing we can never get back. For this very reason, how we spend our time reflects what's most important to us.

Never is this statement truer than when we are in a relationship. I'll be the first to agree that spending time with your man is very important! How else are you going to get to know each other? Nonetheless, not establishing any boundaries or limits to our time for a man who is not our husband is an open invitation for sin to slither into lives.

Here are ways in which we single women who date may choose to spend our time that can take us out of the will of God. Oh, and before you read them, just know there's no finger-pointing here! I have been guilty of all of these things as well.

- We stop going to Bible study because the man we have a crush on thinks going to church during the week is too much.
- Due to all those late-night discussions with a guy who has suddenly become the center of our world, we no longer have the motivation to get up early in the mornings to study the Word of God before our day begins.
- We stop volunteering with ministries that we previously loved and were fully committed to because he believes it "shouldn't take all that" when it comes

to serving the Lord.

- We stop working out (or better yet honoring our temple) because the man we now adore believes we should have more flexibility to spend time with him.

Like it or not, anything or anyone that we allow to compromise our worship time with God becomes our idol. Now, let's not get crazy! I'm not saying we should be in church from sunup to sundown. Our lives must maintain a healthy balance, no matter what. *An idol is simply anything or anyone that we seek or try to please more than our Lord and Savior, Jesus Christ.*

Another definition of an idol is a *"person, place, or thing that is used as an object of worship."* Make no mistake, an idol can be anything! Examples may include a workout routine, supervisor, job, car, money, home, designer clothes, child, mother, father, husband, boyfriend, girlfriends, the lottery, an organization, etc.

I confess to having had many idols throughout my life. How else would I be able to write from such a personal point of view? Quite frankly, I probably would have remained that way too, if God had not broken me. Unfortunately, He had to do it time and time again before I truly learned. He had to remind me of His first commandment, which says, in Exodus 20:3, "You shall have no other gods before me." Now, I'm thankful that I finally understand the importance of this lesson while still in the natural world of the living as opposed to the supernatural one of the unknown.

Psssst, want to know a secret, ladies? As far as most men are concerned, they seldom want us to make them our idol! A lot of times we simply do it without needing to be asked.

Hands down, time is an essential pathway to relationships. Nevertheless, when dating we should never allow a wide-open road of access to our time. We should instead set up occasional

❧ Your Reflection Pool ❧

speed bumps to ensure that our journey together is slow and insightful. Most importantly, we must allow the voice of God to serve as our navigation system, providing directions on which way we should go.

The second aspect affecting our relational lives is *home*. They say home is where the heart is. This is certainly true! When we fall in love, it's our natural tendency to share our nesting space with the man we love.

The problem occurs when every moment of your home life revolves around a man who is not your husband—i.e., he's always at your home or you're always at his. When it gets to a point where he has drawer space in your dresser, he has become your play husband. The Lord might have excused this when we were kids, but definitely not when we are grown adults! Not your husband, but you have his name on your checking and savings account? Not your husband, but you're spending the weekend at his house? Not your husband, but he knows how much you are getting back on your taxes? Not your husband, but you need to ask his permission before going on a trip with your friends? Not your husband, but his name is tattooed on your body?

I'm sure many of us single women have caused the Lord to shake His head in frustration over our actions regarding men. I rejoice that we don't have to continue that way! How do you remedy this type of mindset? There are three simple ways: First, pray and ask the Holy Spirit daily to reveal to you which boundaries you should set in place when dating. Secondly, consistently meditate on the Word of God. And lastly, keep this book to remind you of why it's important to keep your focus.

Our third ingredient is "*Money, Money, Money, Mon . . . eeeey!*" It goes without saying that money is important, and there's nothing wrong with having it as long as we don't love or worship it. First Timothy 6:10 tells us, "for the love of money is a root of all kinds of evil.

Some people, eager for money, have wandered from the faith and pierced themselves with many griefs."

What we spend our money on shows where it ranks in our lives. Buying things for those we love is a natural tendency. The Word even supports this virtue. Acts 20:35b reminds us, "It is more blessed to give than to receive." Blessing our man with thoughtful presents is a considerate thing to do. Nevertheless, we should pump the brakes when the gift-giving is one-sided. Even when it is not, we should always proceed with caution when buying for a man who's not our husband. Turn to any TV court show, and you're likely to see a woman suing her former boyfriend for repayment on a purchased item or cash loan. It's always the same sad pattern: woman meets man, he blows her mind in a short period of time, man requests an item or money, woman provides it to him, relationship ends . . . and she tries to sue for repayment. Of course, these types of lawsuits

❧ Your Reflection Pool ❧

occur between former married couples as well, but the truth is most people, and judges for that matter, can see why we would want to give an extravagant gift to a husband. It's hard to defend ourselves in a court of law when the case involves a man who has no legal obligation to us. Without fail, the judge will advise the woman to make better choices next time.

Always buying his kids school clothes is also dangerous. So you've been together for many years—great. You've known those kids since they were babies, gotcha. "But I love those kids as if they were my own"—got it. Sharing our hard-earned money year after year with a man who won't honor us before God as his wife is asking for trouble. Again, why play the role of wife if he won't respect you enough to make you one? Beloved, God created us to be originals, not man-made copies.

The fourth category is *sex*. I confess this one has been the biggest challenge for me, and I wouldn't be surprised if others feel the same way as well! As females, most of us are affectionate by nature. Oftentimes when we fall in love, we want to share our love through sexual intimacy. We don't always realize that real intimacy starts with the mind. How else can you discover who a man is unless you get to know how him as a person first?

It's only when we have a carnal mind that we react through our flesh. *The definition of "carnal" is sensual or sexual.* Most of what we see on TV has a carnal message, even the commercials. If it's not the woman in the shower washing her hair while moaning "yes, yes, yes!", it's the woodsy hulk who suddenly appears when the housewife simply needs a roll of paper towels to clean her kitchen. Sexual undertones are everywhere. The world pulses with the theme that sex sells. It also creates soul ties. Never heard of them? Allow me to explain.

According to *Charisma Magazine,* a *soul tie is an ungodly spiritual link that is shared between two people after they have sex.* This should not be confused with finding a soul mate or destined mate. *A soul mate or destined mate* (as I like to call them) *is the result when two people are ordained by God for each other. A soul tie, on the other hand, is an unclean linkage that occurs as the result of sin. Each time we have sex with someone who is not our spouse, it creates a sinful blemish on our spirit.* A *blemish* is *"a mark or imperfection that spoils the appearance."* Another definition says, *"something that spoils a person's reputation or good record."* In other words, by having sex outside of marriage, it dishonors our bodily temple and grieves the Holy Spirit within us.

That's why God says in Ephesians 5:25–27, "Husbands, love your wives, just as Christ loved the church and gave himself up for her to make her holy, cleansing her by the washing with water through the word, and present her to himself as a radiant church, without a stain or wrinkle or any, but holy and blameless." Still think we can justify having sex with a man who

Your Reflection Pool

is not our husband? How about Ephesians 5:3, which says, "But among you there must not be even a hint of sexual immorality, or of any kind of impurity, or of greed, because these are improper for God's holy people."

Don't be fooled by what the world is telling you! God warns us in Ephesians 5:6–7, "Let no one deceive you with empty words, for because of such things God's wrath comes on those who are disobedient. Therefore, do not be partners with them." So for anyone who conveniently claims to have a "life partner" even though no marriage has occurred, they are "deceiving you with empty words," and that is "improper for God's holy people."

The fifth and final aspect of a woman's life in relationship is *gifts*. Each of us has natural gifts that make us who we are. Some young ladies have a talent for singing, while others have a passion for playing an instrument. Others may be great at managing money. Then there are those who can flawlessly organize a dinner party. The Lord may have blessed you to be an exceptional cook or brilliant decorator.

Whatever your gifts, each woman has her own. Our gifts are to be used for kingdom building and as helpers to our spouses—not the man we've just lived with for the past four years. Remember Genesis 2:18: "The LORD God said, 'It is not good for the man to be alone. I will make a helper suitable for him.'" That man, of course, was Adam, who is also referred to as *husband*. That helper is Eve, who in the same story is later called *wife*. As a reminder, Ephesians 5:24 says, "Now as the church submits to Christ, so also wives should submit to their husbands in *everything*." Ultimately, *everything* that we have to offer is designated only for the man who God has ordained as our husband.

The Unwed Approach versus The Married Wife

Now that we've identified all five

relationship factors, let's try a simple and quick exercise to see how we're doing in the "unwed" versus "married" lifestyle choice. Are you up for the challenge? Awesome, then let's begin! Please grab a piece of paper and fold it in half. On *both* sides of the paper, write down the following categories of a woman's life:

Side A	Side B

1. **Time**
2. **Home**
3. **Money**
4. **Sex**
5. **Gifts**

Label one side of the folded paper Side A and the other Side B. On one side, write down everything you do for and with your boyfriend *on a weekly basis*. On the opposite side, write down everything that you *would do* for and with your future husband *on a weekly basis*. Hopefully, both sides are not identical!

There should be a *clear* distinction between what you will do for a husband and what you do for a boyfriend. When we treat a boyfriend like a husband, our actions tell him that he doesn't need to honor us as his wife. That we're fine with whatever commitment level *he decides* to give us. Today, unwed wives are such a norm that it's becoming more and more rare when a woman decides not to become one.

To prove my point, let's turn to Hollywood. Here are some of the world's most beautiful women, many of whom have reached the coveted status of movie star. One would easily agree these women are gorgeous, rich, successful, and famous. Sadly, many of these privileged women have settled for being baby mamas. The music industry is no exception. There are many Grammy Award winners who have children, but no husbands.

Please understand, it's not my intent to judge. I have indicated throughout this book that the path of righteousness was so far from my daily walk, I would have needed a map and a bulldozer to find it. I've learned, beloved, that we should never mind confessing our faults. That's when the Holy Spirit can minister to our weaknesses!

Paul understood this better than most, which is why he wrote the following Scripture:

> "But he said to me, 'My grace is sufficient for you, for my power is made perfect in weakness.' Therefore, I will boast all the more gladly about my weaknesses, so that

~ Your Reflection Pool ~

> Christ's power may rest on me. That is why, for Christ's sake, I delight in weaknesses, in insults, in hardships, in persecutions, in difficulties. For when I am weak, then I am strong." 2 Corinthians 12:9–10

There are those of us who humbly want to please the Lord above all else. When that is the case, the most challenging thing can be living according to His will. But we must learn to do so if we are to be obedient. I struggle daily. I know how much pressure it can be when you stop having or refuse to have sex with the man you love. I understand how it hurts to think of him being with someone else. It becomes even more painful if he distances himself from you. He may even throw it in your face that you left him no choice, since you are not "taking care of his needs." This can make you feel like you are being punished for trying to live a life that pleases God.

Please be encouraged, dearest. We will never *fail* when we put the Lord first! I don't care how fine he is or how good in bed. A man whose words and actions do not line up with the Holy Word will cause us to be separated from our Creator. May God have mercy on us when we deliberately choose ungodly wants over His will! Matthew 10:28 says, "Do not be afraid of those who kill the body but cannot kill the soul. Rather, be afraid of the One who can destroy both soul and body in hell."

Don't be deceived. Just because that brother grew up in the church or is on the ministerial staff does not mean he is the one God has chosen for you. That includes the man you met at church who said, "God told me that you are going to be my wife." I can't tell you how many times I've personally heard that statement! None of those men were sent to me by God. Want to know how I know? None of their actions lined up with the true character of a man of valor. By silently observing them and the type of decisions they made over time, I was able to discern the truth.

I once met a very attractive man who told me I was meant to be his wife. Even though we became friends, my Heavenly Father never confirmed his claim with my spirit. Consequently, I told him I simply wanted to be friends. For some reason, that seemed to make him more determined to prove me (and God, I guess) wrong.

One night while we were talking on the phone, I mentioned that the Lord had revealed to me that part of my ordained purpose was to finish and publish this book. I was shocked and taken aback when he sternly told me that once I became his wife, I wouldn't "have time for that pipe dream." He went on to say, "I'm glad you don't have any kids so I don't have to worry about any baby daddy drama. You will only have time for me and my girls." I thought to myself, *Yeah . . . that's exactly what I was NOT thinking*.

Your Reflection Pool

Thankfully, I was able to end that association swiftly. As the late great poet Maya Angelou once said, “When someone shows you who they are, believe them; the first time.” It should go without saying that the standard we hold men to, we should equally hold ourselves accountable to. If we don’t want a love interest who doesn’t see the value of our God-given gifts and talents, then we should never belittle his either.

Ultimately, we have to pray and ask the Lord for the wisdom to discern our destined mate. If we’re not careful, it’s easy to fall for the trap of a counterfeit. Think about criminals who create fake money. Sometimes, only special agencies can distinguish a copy from an original. Our Lord Jesus Christ does not deal with forged copies. He only approves original designs. Don’t believe me? We live in a world of over seven and a half billion people and yet, no one on the face of this earth is quite like you! I, for instance, love all creative aspects of life.

Art inspires me. I am moved when I hear the haunting, classical notes of eighteenth-century Black composer, Joseph Boulogne, Le Chevalier de Saint-Georges. He not only played with French Queen Marie Antoinette, but he also inspired the legendary composer Wolfgang Amadeus Mozart. I become spellbound when viewing paintings by artist Tamara Natalie Madden. Photography by Gordon Parks simply captivates me. Glass sculptures by Dale Chihuly take my breath away. Authors Alexandre Dumas and Harper Lee are two of my literary heroes. No one can argue the talents of Leonardo da Vinci and Michelangelo Buonarroti. And yet, none of these geniuses could have ever created the greatest masterpiece of all time, the human body. Only our Heavenly Father deserves this distinction. That's how awesome He is! He not only created each of us as a priceless original, but He made us to be in fellowship with Him. In addition, He blessed us with the Holy Spirit, who is our bridge to the presence of God.

Ever wonder why we feel so guilty once we get saved and then backslide into sin? Our spirit wrestles with our flesh when we are disobedient. Imagine if you had two grown people fighting in your room all night while you were trying to rest. It's safe to say you wouldn't get much sleep! That's what happens to us in the supernatural realm when we sin. Our spirit is trying to win against our flesh. When we continue to sin, more power is added to the flesh. Eventually, our spirit woman becomes defeated. Sadly, she is then tortured by our flesh when her only goal is to save us from eternal damnation.

In John 14:6, Jesus said, "I am the way and the truth and the life." He created the Holy Spirit to help us walk with Him and discern truth from falsehood. Part of that is the ability to recognize a true man or woman of God from an imposter. How can we tell if they are imposters? A true man or woman of God will not contradict the Word, whereas a phony will make up

Your Reflection Pool

excuses as to why we should disobey it solely for the purposes of their own agenda. For instance, I once had a guy try to tell me that unmarried men and women are supposed to have sex before they decide to marry. What was his excuse? So that you can test each other out. Of course, he couldn't show me any proof of that in the Bible. I was able to easily disregard his claim. A real man of God will be revealed through his actions, not by crafty words.

Points to Remember

- ❐ Time is the most precious resource in a woman's life.
- ❐ A soul tie is a shackle upon our spirit. It stays with us long after the moment of sin has passed.
- ❐ The only one we are supposed to share our all-in-all with is God first, then our husband.

Finished Reading Chapter 5? *Collect Your 5th Red Diamond.*

If what we are willing to share with a boyfriend is identical to what we would share with our husband, then we are out of order according to God's will.

6

The Four Principles of Courting Versus Dating

"Only a gentleman knows the difference between the romance of courtship versus simply dating."

—Tashma White

Sweet sister, I have a very important question that I'd like to ask you. Before I do, though, please understand it is in no way intended to offend or degrade you. It is instead one that may inspire you to evaluate how you present yourself to men. Okay, so what's this important question that I want to ask you? It is . . . *Are you court worthy?* Meaning, do you behave in a way that a man would want to court you?

Your immediate response may be "Of course I am!" But are you really?

In this chapter I will be discussing our presentation of self, as well as the exact difference between courting and dating. If you don't know what I'm talking about, don't worry. You're at the right address, because I didn't either until recently.

Before we define courting, let's talk a little about our cultural context. Believe it or not, we live in a society made for couples. This can have an adverse effect not just on women but on men. How many times have you walked into a fine dining establishment and seen a table set for one? How many vacation specials are marketed for only one person? Valentine's Day is synonymous with love. How many spa discounts for singles have you run across for that day? Plenty of people who are single want to pamper themselves, but they are oftentimes overlooked. All of this adds up to a lot of pressure for women: *get a date, find a man, become part of a couple, fast*.

Well, in the same way a single woman may feel societal pressures, so can a man. That's why it's important to understand why a man is pursuing you in the first place. Is it to win your exclusive affection and eventually hand in marriage (courting) or is it so he won't be the only guy alone during this year's company party (dating)?

I can hear you thinking out loud. *What's wrong with a man asking me out just for a date? How else are we going to get to know each other?* The answer is there's nothing wrong with it—but it's important to know how you're each perceiving the date. He may want to get to know you, but why? Is he interested in the possibility of a long-term relationship, or does he just need

~ Your Reflection Pool ~

a space saver for his social calendar?

While you're pondering this question, I want to let you in on a little secret, beloved. The decision to be in a relationship is not only up to him, it's also up to you! Remember my question from earlier? I asked, "*Are you court worthy?*"

There are four basic principles of courting which differ from dating.

Principle #1

Your Actions Will Show Him If You Are Court Worthy or Not—And His Will Do the Same

How do you carry yourself around men? Now, I'm not talking about having your nose so far up in the air that you can barely swallow. What I mean is, are you demonstrating a polite (not desperate) demeanor? Does your style of dress say tasteful or tasteless?

My sweet sister, a man may be captivated by our cleavage, but he will not want it displayed in front of those he respects most (e.g., his mother, father, sister, or pastor). The way we present ourselves will determine whether a man deems us "court worthy." Sure, there are plenty of women out there who dress in a way that leaves little to the imagination, and they still end up married. Nonetheless, my darling friend, this book is for those of us who have a desire to date with a godly consciousness, not a worldly one.

When we decide to wait on the Lord for our future spouse, we must understand that He is not going to make a random selection. Your gift will be tailor-fit for you. Any man can propose, buy a ring, rent the tux, and say, "I do!" But there's a glacier-sized distinction between a *stand-in male* and a *stand-up man.*

Here's the difference. *The stand-in male is the one who stands in the place of your true destined mate.* His pursuit of a woman is not driven by a commitment to the will of God but by a self-serving need (he may need a place to stay, your car for transportation, your paycheck to pay his bills, etc.) Targeting lonely women is as common to him as shopping at the local discount store. He knows that desperate women will settle for anyone and anything—ammunition that he uses to his advantage. He simply takes up space by helping our cold beds feel more inviting at night. His only real contribution to us is changing our reservation status and taking our apartment from single to double occupancy.

A stand-in male can be encountered anywhere at any time. I was in a store one time and a man came up to me and said, "Today must be your birthday. If you want a real gift, take me home." I chuckled and politely told him, "No, thank you." I smiled and moved on down the aisle. A few minutes later, he came to me again and said, "You're sure?" Curiously, I cocked my head to the side, smiled, and sincerely asked, "Does that line really work with women?" He looked startled at my blunt question and replied, "Sometimes, yes."

Your Reflection Pool

"Wow," I said. "Have a blessed day, my brother." He smiled and returned, "You too!" As I later drove home, I thought about the women he had won by his practiced routine. Now, let's be clear. We women can be notorious flatterers as well. Why clean one side of a room if both sides are untidy? Fact is, we all want and deserve to be loved. Some of us just go about it the wrong the way, like I used to do.

Now, let's discuss the stand-up man, shall we? The reason he's called a *stand-up man* is that *he stands up for you when you need him most. He won't tolerate another human disrespecting you. This man will cherish your heart, not crush it.* Most importantly, it is the Holy Spirit that guides his life, not the immature jests of his friends. He accompanies his woman to church instead of sending her off with a demand that she better be back home soon. A stand-up man marries a woman before getting her pregnant. He will stand up with you at the altar before God and family to make you his bride, not just his live-in lover.

Believe me when I say, our Heavenly Father wants stand-up men for His precious, upright daughters, rather than substitute stand-in males. And guess what? We can have one, when we decide to wait on the Savior. The treasure He will grant us will be priceless compared to the fool's gold we can find in abundance when we're outside His will.

Principle #2

His Mind Is Already Made Up About You Being a Worthy Long-Term Investment

When a man truly wants to court you, he has already deemed you court worthy. You are significant to his life. You won't have to ask how he feels about you; his actions will show you. His introduction of you will change from standard to personal. It will no longer just be, *"This is Kyndle."* It will suddenly transform into, *"This is my special lady, Kyndle."* He'll ask for and value your opinion before he makes a serious decision.

I was once seeing a guy who inquired about my favorite color. About a week or so later, I was shocked to see that same color had been incorporated into some of his home decor. I knew I didn't love him, and I wasn't willing to settle—so ultimately we didn't stay together. Nonetheless, I have never forgotten the thoughtfulness of his gesture.

When a man is only dating you, he might not necessarily care what your favorite colors are. In his mind, your association is not a permanent arrangement. You may be his Friday night girl while someone else is Saturday. Hence the reason he won't infuse aspects of your personality into his personal space. He certainly doesn't subscribe to the notion that "mi casa es su casa."

Now, it's not only about a man considering *your* potential. Dear heart, it is imperative for you to evaluate whether or not *he* is also worthy of your time! A true courtship is as much about

Your Reflection Pool

you as it is about him. It always saddens me to see a beautiful, gifted sister in Christ willingly place herself on the shelf in the hopes that a particular man will decide to marry her. Oftentimes, things on shelves have an expiration date. That's how it can be when we place our heart on hold for a man. We give up the freshness of our youth, all because we are trying to prove to him that we are worthy of his marriage proposal.

Now, let's stop here for a moment. As I've said before, it is not my intent to rush anyone into marriage—not at all. It's one thing if you want to travel for a while, get an education, or take the time to find yourself. That's a totally different scenario from you wanting to get married but are waiting on a boyfriend who is still dancing around the issue years later. Please don't waste the time God has given you. Let that man be impressed with the fact that you have a content and meaningful life. Show him that it is he who must to try to keep up with you, not the other way around.

Principle #3
He Will Initiate Introducing You to Those He Respects Most

True courtship requires your involvement not only in his life but in his family's as well. In a true courtship, you will never have to ask, "When am I going to meet your mother?" He will take the initiative and invite you.

Now that I'm older and wiser, I will never again allow a man to meet my mother before I meet his (or his closest relatives). Is this some type of dating rule or game tactic, you might wonder? Let me assure you, it is not. Consider my point from this angle: it speaks volumes when a man wants to take you home to meet his family. (If he doesn't have a relationship with his immediate family for some reason, then he should want you to meet his extended one.) Until you meet either group, you'd better categorize that relationship as casually dating.

I can't tell you the number of women I know who've been with a man for years, some have even had children with him, and yet they have never once met his mother or closest relatives. Ladies, a true gentleman demonstrates his feelings with honorable actions, not just with sweet but empty promises. Most importantly, he will do it in a relatively short period of time. Now, I'm not talking about three months, but I'm not referring to anything more than three years either. Why become serious with someone who won't take you home to meet those he loves? It's one thing if he doesn't associate with them. It's another ball game if he does spend time with them but he hasn't asked you to do the same.

We mustn't forget that a stand-up man speaks with his actions, while the stand-in male always leaves enough room to exit the relationship. He's here today, most likely gone tomorrow. Never offer a man an honor that he is not willing to extend to you. Only after you've

❧ Your Reflection Pool ❧

met his family should you bestow on him the privilege of meeting your own.

Principle #4
His Actions Will Assure You That Your Future Is Secure with Him

Taking care of business is what grown, mature men and women do. For example, my parents divorced when my brother and I were young. Although we were very poor, my mother taught us to be grateful for God's blessings. Growing up, my brother never had a male role model to mentor him. He certainly didn't have anyone to show him how to service a car, mow the lawn, cut his own hair, fix things around the house, etc. Through the grace of God, he took the initiative to seek out and learn how to do those things for himself and for our family. Nowadays, he's still taking care of things, not only for our mother but also for his own wife and children. Although he works full-time, his children have grown up witnessing him growing his own vegetables, remodeling rooms in their home, beautifying their lawn with flowers and shrubbery, and watching out for them in every way. Don't get me wrong—he's far from perfect, just like you and me. Even so, I'm thankful to Almighty God that he demonstrates to his daughters and son how a responsible man is supposed to take care of his family.

As women, the same rule should apply to us as well. Many successful and highly driven men desire a woman who is a go-getter in her own right. When it's obvious that we contribute to society, that is attractive to a secure man with aspirations. It shows him that we too know how to handle our own business.

Healthy courtships are built on mutual respect. When a man courts you, everyone close to him knows where he stands in relation to his feelings for you. His devotion to you will be evident to your family and his long before your names ever appear jointly on a marriage certificate. That's how he will assure you that your future is secure with him. That's one of the major differences between courting and dating.

So what happens when you meet your destined mate? Should you become engaged? Remember, the purpose of this book is not to rush you into marriage. It is, instead, to give you some insight into what dating with a godly purpose can and should look like. If you meet someone you think you would want to spend the rest of your life with, here are some insightful questions that you might want to consider first.

Questions for a Deeper Relationship (Pre-Engagement)

- Are you saved?
- If we ever considered marriage, how often would you attend Bible study or church with me?
- How often do you think we should pray together as a couple, if ever?
- Would you serve in ministry with me? If

so, which area of ministry?

- How would our relationship affect my / your / our children?
- What is your idea of a "good wife?"
- How would you prioritize the following list? (Number **1 = Most Important** to Number **12 = Least Important**):
    - God, children, best friend(s), wife, parents, mother of your child(ren), family vacations, romantic getaways, your wife's birthday, weekly date night, night out with your boys, your own private time
- What type of role model will you be for my son or daughter?
- What type of role model would you expect me to be for your son or daughter?
- What type of relationship will you have with my parents, siblings, and friends?
- What type of relationship will you

expect for me to have with your parents, siblings, and friends?

- Are you good at saving money?
- How often do you save money? (Be sure to pay attention to the answer!)
- Do you maintain your savings, or do you spend it frequently? (You won't think this question matters until this affects your quality of life in the future!)
- What's your philosophy on spending money from your savings?
- Whose responsibility will it be to make sure the household bills are paid? If so, in what way? What is your philosophy on paying bills together?
- Do you owe any back taxes? If so, from which years, and how much?
- Would you be willing to exchange credit reports before we announce our engagement? If not, why not? Do you see credit as essential to our financial future?

- Would we file taxes together or separately?
- What is your definition of "helping out around the house"?
- What role would you play in maintaining our home (lawn care, repairs, etc.)?
- How often would I need to expect your family or friends to visit?
- How do you feel about me occasionally spending time with my girlfriends? What about an occasional weekend trip?
- How much time do you prefer to spend with your friends?
- How many times would you expect me to cook each week? Does that include breakfast and weekends?
- How many times would you be willing to cook each week? Does that include breakfast and weekends?
- How many times would you prefer to have sex each week?
- How will we manage our family health

insurance (together or separately)?

- What are your deal breakers when it comes to marriage?
- What are your pet peeves when living with someone?

Seems like a lot of questions, doesn't it? Well, let me tell you, marriage is serious business. A beautiful and joyous business, but serious no less. Unfortunately, a lot of people don't realize that until after they are in it. Why waste time with someone who can't be bothered to answer these insightful questions about your future together? Better to be on one page during the courtship than on two separate bookends after the wedding. In case you're wondering why I said *bookends,* it's because they are always facing in the opposite direction!

I'm now convinced that a lot of dead-end relationships could be avoided *if* we had the right discussions beforehand. That's why celibacy during courtship is so essential! It

❧ Your Reflection Pool ❧

allows you to get to know each other as friends long before you become lovers. When we truly seek the guidance of the Holy Spirit, a relationship is a beautiful thing to behold. But when holy matrimony is entered into for the wrong reasons (i.e., just to satisfy lust or loneliness), you may find yourself living on a merry-go-round nightmare. Marriage expectations should be one of the most serious conversations you ever have in your life. I didn't understand that my first time around. Trust me . . . *now I do!*

Regardless of whether you've made a trip to the altar before or not, one truth remains the same. We must truly seek healing, forgiveness, and wisdom from the Holy Spirit in order to avoid numerous repeat visits in the future.

Points to Remember

❒ It is our actions, not our words, that will best indicate to a man if we are court worthy or not.

❒ Desperation is as much of a turnoff to men as it is to us.

❒ A stand-in man takes up space in your life for his own self-serving purposes.

❒ A stand-up man stands up for you before God, your family, and your friends.

Finished Reading Chapter 6? *Collect Your 6th Red Diamond.*

We should never wait for our mate to arrive before having a reason to enjoy and celebrate life. God should always be our first source of joy and peace.

7

What Type of Food Are You?

"Few things smell sweeter unto the Lord than when we glisten with the fruits of the Spirit."
—Tashma White

I have arrived at a theory that single women resemble certain foods. Just as food can be categorized in different ways, so can we. In this case, I see four basic types we can fall into.

The first type of single women is similar to

a snack. A *"Snack-Style Woman"* or *SSW is considered a tasty treat to a man. Her looks may be visually pleasing, but there isn't much substance for relationship with her.* A "snack" is an easy-to-prepare food eaten in place of a regular meal or between regular meals. Another definition is *any sort* of food suitable for eating. The words that most capture my attention are "easy" and "any sort." The SSW, once sampled, is easily forgotten. A man will think nothing of leaving her, because his connection to her is only on a superficial basis. They may share sex, but they have no mutual emotional bond or commitment.

When there's no emotional attachment for a man, he is less likely to treat a woman with respect. Thus, he'll treat this type of woman like any stranger off the street. As "easy" as it was for him to capture her, it will be even easier to get rid of her.

From her own perspective, the SSW is determined to find love no matter what.

Therefore, she willingly gives all she has to offer without the slightest hesitation. She's as diligent as someone looking for a shoe to match a particular outfit. The problem with the SSW is that after years of searching, she may still come up empty-handed.

These women refuse to wait on God for love. In their minds, He's not moving fast enough. Many have convinced themselves that they should be married by a certain age. When that time comes and goes, they lose faith in ever finding true love. This is dangerous, because it's like telling God, "Yeah, Lord, I know You are great and all, but I don't trust that You are capable of creating my destined mate." A destined mate is a man whom the Lord has custom-made just for you. Furthermore, God has a divinely appointed time for him to meet you.

The ultimate problem with an SSW is she's likely to take matters of the heart into her own hands. She would rather trust (and sometimes

Your Reflection Pool

pay) a company of strangers to help her find what she desires most, love. Now, I'm not saying online dating is not good. I know several couples who met online years ago and are still in love today. Nonetheless, my goal is to encourage you to "Have faith in God" (Mark 11: 22a), no matter what has yet to happen in your love life.

Don't forget there are over seven and a half billion people in this world. That means even after we weed out the Down Low brothers, the crazy, the lazy, the abusive, drug users or dealers, gamblers, porn addicts, sexual deviants, con artists, cheaters, child molesters and abusers, the selfish, the inconsiderate, players (either in church or on the streets), murderers, rapists, mama's boys, the self-serving, and the sexists, there are *still* enough good, eligible men to go around! That's why we must look to God to guide our destined mate to us, not man-made sources. Who better to recognize real love than the One who gave His life for it? We never have to use our bodies as a quick snack for a man in the hopes of trying to gain love. Simply trust the Sacred One who paid the ultimate sacrifice for us, confirming we are already loved.

The next type of single woman is the *Appetizer-Style Woman* or *ASW.* Appetizers are more filling than snacks, but they still won't satisfy a grown man for too long. One definition of an appetizer is *"a small dish of food served at the beginning of a meal to stimulate the appetite."* Notice the important phrases here: "at the beginning" and "to stimulate."

The ASW gets a solid hold of her man *"at the beginning" of the relationship by "stimulating" his interest.* Most us have known an "It Couple" who dated, then unexpectedly broke up. Oddly enough, that same man typically marries the very next woman he dates. It could have been that he was not ready for marriage before. On the other hand, as one of my good

male friends once put it, it might have been

the case that "She simply wasn't wife material." You see, an Appetizer-Style Woman is very appealing to a man, but only for a period of time. Although he may even play house with her for a while, he won't ask her to marry him. He believes she will never make the grade for marriage. Somehow or other, he's come to the conclusion that she doesn't possess the qualities he wants in a wife. She might be a nasty housekeeper, fails to pay her bills on time, shops more than she saves, embarrasses him in front of his friends, doesn't get along with his family, isn't respectful of his mother—any number of things may be off-putting to him here. Whatever the reason, an ASW will only whet a man's appetite—never quite satisfying it. She simply holds him over until what he really wants comes along.

The ASW lives her life by a higher standard than that of the SSW, but her lack of self-discipline or self-control will eventually push her man away. Self-discipline is important in the

Your Reflection Pool

body of Christ. Quite frankly, I'm forty-seven years old, and I am just learning how essential it is to my life! That's why it is a fruit of the Spirit (see the full list on the next page). These are characteristics that all believers should demonstrate in their lives.

It takes pure self-control not to be an unwed wife. It's easy to demonstrate everything we have to offer to the man we love. The hard part is saving the best for only our husband. When we show self-control and self-respect, a man will have no choice but to honor these virtues, thus distinguishing us from other women.

The third category is the *DSW.* No, not the shoe franchise! This stands for *Dessert-Style Woman.* A DSW is a *woman who suffocates her man through clinginess and insecurity.* Just like the calories in most desserts, she can be overwhelming after a while. Experts believe there are over one billion dessert recipes worldwide. From carrot cake to chocolate raspberry torte, the choices are endless. Most of us have our favorites—but how many men want to eat dessert day in and day out? The DSW is extremely needy and tiring. The thought of giving her man some much-needed space never even crosses her mind. Instead, she begins to suffocate him with her need for constant attention.

Human beings have enjoyed desserts since ancient times when we occasionally rolled fruit or nuts in honey. A DSW not only believes she can keep her man with emotional honey, she drowns him in it. But imagine if your man loves chocolate cake, and you feed it to him for three to twelve hours a day. Eventually, the richness of the chocolate will overstimulate his senses. Before you know it, he'll soon grow tired of his favorite dessert and may stop eating it altogether. When we don't give a man some breathing room, he will start to get overwhelmed by our presence. We purposely try to hold on to him with a tight grip, only to feel him slip away anyway through our fingers, on to someone else.

The final type is the *Full-Course-Meal Woman or FCMW.* A full-course meal is a dinner consisting of multiple dishes. In its simplest form, it can consist of three or four foods, such as soup, salad, meat, and dessert. In formal dining, a full-course dinner may include from five to twenty-one courses. In these formalized settings the courses are carefully planned to complement each other. The dishes are smaller and spread out over a long evening, up to three, four, or five hours. The grab words in these definitions are *multiple, carefully planned to complement each other,* and *spread out*.

When a woman is a full-course meal, she's able to present multiple aspects of her life. A FCMW is *a secure woman who is fulfilled first through Christ and then her own personal work, interests, and hobbies*. She understands the value of personal space because she requires it from time to time herself. He is not

❧ Your Reflection Pool ❧

overwhelmed with the pressure of having to be her only source for happiness and entertainment. She desires the presence of our Heavenly Father first and foremost.

When God is the head of our life, all other areas will line up. God's daughter shouldn't be bitter, insecure, nagging, or anxious. If that guy prefers a hamburger Happy Meal to your roasted chicken, sautéed seasoned veggies, homemade garlic mashed potatoes, buttery corn on the cob, cheddar jalapeño cornbread, blueberry lemon pound cake, and sweet tea (I did say I like to cook?), then let him go. If you've got a vegetarian style, and he only wants a tough steak, greasy French fries and Twinkies, perhaps you should pack up your tofu spaghetti balls over creamy noodles, garden salad, garlic parmesan breadsticks, and vegan raspberry buttercream cake and move on with your life.

Now, wait a minute. I'm not saying if a man doesn't like your cooking, get rid of him! This is a metaphor for our lives. When we mature into a

Full-Course-Meal Woman, we leave nothing to be desired. Therefore, a man with a "limited palate" (accustomed to dating women completely the opposite of you) may not be able to appreciate what you have to offer. He may only like processed foods, not gourmet dishes made from the finest ingredients. If that's the case, let him go.

Now, to be fair, the same also applies to us, beloved. If we meet a godly man who does not bring drama and cheating games into our lives, and yet that's what we thrive on the most, then we do not deserve his time or affection either.

As daughters of Christ, we should shine like a lighthouse on a dark night. Most importantly, we should reflect the fruits of the Spirit. These are identified in Galatians 5:22: *"But the Fruit of the Spirit is love, joy, peace, patience, kindness, goodness, faithfulness, gentleness and self-control."*

The Spiritual Nutrients of a FCMW

Serving Size 1 (Lifetime Supply of Jesus Christ)

Amount Per Serving	% **Daily Value***
Repentance of Sin	100% Forgiven
Humbleness	100% Saturated with the Holy Spirit
Trusting in the Lord	100% Protected
Obedience to God's Word	100% Favored by God
Seeking God's Will	100% Anointed
Daily Prayer and Worship Life	100% Delivered
Asking God for Wisdom	100% Grace
Fasting for a Cause	100% Breakthrough
Studying and Meditating on God's Word	100% Relationship with God
Let Go, Let God!	100% Peaceful
Honoring God with the Life We Live	100% Pleasing to the Lord
Praising the One True, Living God	100% Attracts God's Attention
Resist the Temptation of Sin	100% Reward of Eternal Life
Self-Control	100% Good Steward of God's Blessings
Pleading the Blood Jesus Christ	100% Victory Over Satan's Schemes

*The Percent Daily Values are based on a Born-Again Daughter of Jesus Christ

Single or married, we should aspire to be Full-Course-Meal Women as daughters of Jesus Christ. Once we marry, however, there's an even higher level of spiritual grace that we should aim to attain.

Proverbs 31 beautifully describes the quintessential woman of God:

> **The Proverbs 31 Woman, or The Wife of Noble Character**
>
> A wife of noble character who can find? She is worth far more than rubies. Her husband has full confidence in her and lacks nothing of value. She brings him good, not harm, all the days of her life.
>
> She selects wool and flax and works with eager hands. She is like the merchant ships, bringing her food from afar. She gets up while it is still dark; she provides food for her family and portions for her servant girls.
>
> She considers a field and buys it; out of her earrings she plants a vineyard. She sets about her work vigorously; her arms are strong for her tasks. She sees that her

trading is profitable, and her lamp does not go out at night. In her hand she holds the distaff and grasps the spindle with her fingers.

She opens her arms to the poor and extends her hands to the needy. When it snows, she has no fear for her household; for all of them are clothed in scarlet. She makes coverings for her bed; she is clothed in fine linen and purple. Her husband is respected at the city gate, where he takes his seat among the elders of the land.

She makes linen garments and sells them, and supplies the merchants with sashes. She is clothed with strength and dignity; she can laugh at the days to come. She speaks with wisdom, and faithful instruction is on her tongue. She watches over the affairs of her household and does not eat the bread of idleness.

Her children arise and call her

Your Reflection Pool

> blessed; her husband
> also, and her praises her: Many women do noble things, but you surpass them all. Charm is deceptive, and beauty is fleeting; but a woman who fears the Lord is to be praised. Give her reward she has earned, and let her works bring her praise at the city gate. (Proverbs 31:1–31)

This Scripture describes a noble woman of God taking care of the needs of her family and household. Notice, it says nothing about a partner or a baby daddy. The only man referenced in this passage is a husband. When I was married, I never prayed and asked the Holy Spirit to give me the wisdom to be a Proverbs 31 woman. Selfishly, I was more concerned about what I wanted than what my husband needed. I found many ways to justify myself, but now I realize that was very much out of order. I have confessed this sin to God, repented, and asked Him to forgive me. I even went a step further and asked my ex-husband to forgive me as well.

The first step to being a Proverbs 31 woman (married or not) is asking God for the wisdom to be the women He purposed for us to be. When this is done with sincerity and humbleness, God through the Holy Spirit will gladly answer our prayer.

Points to Remember

❒ Single women resemble certain types of food.

❒ A destined mate is a man whom the Lord has custom-made just for you. Furthermore, God has a divinely appointed time for him to meet you.

❒ A Full-Course-Meal Woman is fulfilled first through Christ, then through her own work, interests, and hobbies.

Finished Reading Chapter 7? ***Collect Your 7th Red Diamond.***

As single Christian women who desire to someday marry, our ultimate goal should first be to line up with becoming a Proverbs 31 woman.

8

So, You've Fallen. Now What?

"Just because we may fall during celibacy shouldn't be an excuse to keep returning to the scene of the accident."

—Tashma White

Disappointment invaded my peace of mind like severe cramps gripping the insides of my stomach. How could I have let this happen? How in the world could I allow myself to end up back here?

What exactly was "here," you may be wondering? It was a decision that later made me feel *tainted . . . ashamed . . . bitter . . . regretful . . . self-loathing!* It's not easy to admit this, but I want you to know that after everything I've told you about, after all my decisions to live a different kind of life moving forward, I broke my vow of celibacy. Yes, I did. Nope, it wasn't forced from me; I willingly gave it up. Celibacy is a precious gift from our Heavenly Father, and I had dedicated it to Him. Then I reneged on my commitment and discarded it like the wrapping foil from a piece of gum. Years of discipline succumbed to the lust of a dead-end fling.

I knew it was wrong. I simply didn't care. I blocked the internal number of the Holy Spirit so I wouldn't receive any of His messages. All that mattered to me at the time was pleasing a man I was infatuated with, and sadly, fulfilling my own selfish desire.

❧ Your Reflection Pool ❧

What I couldn't have known was how much harder the battle would become after I made that decision. Like a drug dealer coaxing a first-time user, Satan whispered to me and said, *"So, now you've fallen, there's no need for you to try to be celibate again."* You talk about a voice of persuasion! At that point I could have walked away from the mess I had intentionally made—or I could continue to turn away from God. Sadly, I chose the latter. Quite frankly, I wanted to. I mean, why wouldn't I? At the time, I was so caught up in what I wanted to do that I no longer carved out personal time with Him. I had stopped writing my weekly devotional blog under the disguise of "being too busy!" I had created it to encourage single women like myself through life's daily struggles. Ironically, I was the one who had allowed my own secret struggle to draw me away from the thing that mattered most, the presence of my Eternal Father. His Holy Word had become an ornament I only touched during Sunday church service.

Remember those old Life Alert commercials for emergency medical bracelets? They featured a senior citizen who had taken a terrible tumble, and she uses an electronic bracelet to call for medical emergency assistance. Once she reaches them, she cries out desperately, "I've fallen, and I can't get up!" Well, if I had made that commercial from a spiritual standpoint during that period of my life, it would have said, *"I've fallen, and I don't want to get up!"* I mean, let's be real. Premarital sex, cheating, shacking, and unwed pregnancies are so common in the church today that anyone who does *not* participate in these things can easily feel like a freak of nature.

The problem is when I acted like that, I disgraced my Heavenly Father's throne. Yes, I know there's no condemnation in Christ. However, we shouldn't use that to justify our sins. If we do happen to fall, it adds more insult to injury when we stubbornly won't admit to our wrongdoing. The good news is there's always a way to get back up after a spiritual fall. The first step involves acknowledging and repenting before our Glorious Creator. The confession below helped me and may prove to be useful to you as well.

A Prayer of Confession

Heavenly Father, I confess that I have recently fornicated. I repent of this sin and ask that You please forgive me. I do want to live a life that pleases You, for You alone are the Author and Finisher of my faith. I don't want to hurt You anymore, but I am really struggling in this area right now. Lord, we both know that I cannot fight this battle on my own. So, I pray, through the Holy Spirit, that You will give me the strength to turn and, most importantly, stay away from this sinful nature. The world would have me believe that this endeavor is not humanly possible. However, there are women and men

> across the globe who have debunked this myth. Please teach me how to do the same. I pray You will restore me back to You, Loving Savior. In the name of Jesus, I pray. Amen.

This confession will help begin the process of deliverance. The reality is, we should all strive do our best to keep the vows that we make to El Shaddai. Ecclesiastes 5:4 warns, "When you make a vow to God, do not delay to fulfill it. He has no pleasure in fools; fulfill your vows." Even still, I am so thankful that we serve a forgiving and merciful Ruler. Should this be an excuse to continue to do wrong? Certainly, not! That's why I'm praying, beloved, that you will be wiser and smarter than I have been. Please understand what has taken me years to learn: it's never worth it.

But in the event that you do slip up, take heart. All is not lost! We can be redeemed from our sins. Acts 3:19 says, "Repent, then, and turn to God, so that your sins may be wiped out, that times of refreshing may come from the Lord." That's why the assumption that "*Since I messed up and had sex, there's no need for me to try to be celibate again*" is false.

As long as we repent, we can be forgiven. Thus, we can renew our vow of celibacy. The key, however, is to make sure we avoid placing ourselves in situations that would tempt us to break our vow of celibacy in the first place. If we do, God will forgive us, but we shouldn't keep doing it.

But Is This Really Such a Big Deal?

Let's be real. Even now, having read most of this book, you may be thinking you don't have a problem with being an unwed wife. You may wonder why I think celibacy is such a big deal in the first place. So let me ask this: would you be willing to go on a couples retreat with your pastor and first lady while openly sharing a hotel room with a man who is not your

Your Reflection Pool

husband? If your answer is no, then why not? It wouldn't bother you if he were your wedded husband, so why does it matter if he's your unwed husband? Do you see where I'm going with this? For anyone who refuses to see my point, that's fine. But for those of us who understand the danger of mocking God, please continue to read.

How can we sleep with a man who is not our husband before God and feel no conviction? I confess, for a long time, I didn't. I conveniently became what I have coined as a Christian sociopath. What's that, you ask? A sociopath is someone with a personality disorder that causes them to lack a conscience. *A Christian sociopath is someone who feels no remorse or conscience when they are disobedient to God's Word.* I confess to being a Christian sociopath during several periods of my life!

Perhaps you too have fallen from a previous commitment to celibacy. Better yet, maybe you want to try celibacy, but you don't think you have the self-control to follow through with it. Wherever you're at, none of us can do it on our own. I truly believe that celibacy is not humanly possible through our own strength. I believe if you are not constantly plugged into the Holy Word and seeking the guidance of the Holy Spirit through prayer, you can forget about it! Abstaining from sex requires much more than our best intentions. *That is why I consider this chapter to be the most important one in the book.* We mere mortals have to understand the importance of standing up again after we've taken a spiritual fall.

My goal is to inspire any woman of any age who has ever broken her vow of celibacy to understand that she can get back on track. Below are five steps that tell us how.

Step 1: We must acknowledge the seriousness of having sex without marriage.

It's easy to tell oneself, "Well, everyone

else is doing it, and God hasn't struck them down. In fact, many of them are prospering. So what if I do the same thing?" In today's world, we tend to justify our lifestyles by what we want, not by what the Lord requires. That's why you are likely to hear someone say, "I could never marry someone without living with them first." Most of us know that sex without marriage is wrong, but we don't care. We may also justify our actions by telling ourselves that the Bible doesn't apply to our life in the world today. But if the Lord is the same yesterday, today, and tomorrow . . . so is His word. Make no mistake, *The Great "I Am That I Am"* will not lower His standards to appease our lifestyle.

First Corinthians 6:9a says, "Do you not know that the wicked will not inherit the Kingdom of God? Do not be deceived: Neither the sexually immoral . . ." The good news is that with Him, forgiveness and a better life are possible. I don't care what happened yesterday or even three minutes ago. All we need is a

Your Reflection Pool

willingness to please the Eternal Creator, first and foremost.

Step 2: Find an Accountability Partner.

You may be on the side of the room where someone would ask, *"Hold up? Is she for real?"* My answer, in turn, is, *"Absolutely, yes!"*

For those of us who want to be obedient to God, being an unwed wife is not a position of honor. We understand that according to His Word, He intended for us to be so much more. Unwed Wife Syndrome is a spiritual disease. It's a by-product of today's society and is accepted and encouraged by most, but the fact is, "unwed wife" is a title that should never be celebrated among daughters of Christ. Giving way to this syndrome could damage not only our spirit woman but most importantly, our relationship with God.

So for those of us who are serious about our relationship with our Creator, I encourage you to consider getting an accountability partner. Now, please don't hand this duty over to just anyone! It is a vital part of your walk with Jesus Christ. That's why the right kind of accountability partner should not beat you down with tactics of shame. He or she should, instead, listen without judging. This person should build you up, not tear you down; uplift you with words of inspiration. And he or she can be there when you need someone to call and say, "Help me, I'm facing temptation!"

The majority of us have "That Name" that, when it pops up on our phone, makes our eyes light up and heart jump. However, if "That Name" is calling you for no other reason than a quick hookup, do yourself a favor and ignore it. Now . . . don't tell me you can't, because I know that you can. Set your mind on honoring God, and He will help you flee that temptation. And better yet—help yourself honor God by getting an accountability partner to help you flee!

My sista, I'm telling you what I've learned

and had to do myself, not just giving you advice because it sounds good. We are adored by the Most High God. Fornication hurts Him. Our Holy Father created our temple (our body) for a purpose. Aren't temples sacred monuments? Beloved, a man will only respect our temples when we behave in a way that requires it.

Step 3: Close Your Gates.

Our "gates" are the areas of our body through which we receive or interpret information—in other words, our ears and eyes. There are certain love songs, movies, and novels that I can no longer entertain, because they make me more susceptible to falling into sin. Sound extreme? Maybe so. All I can tell you is once our gates are closed to worldly influences that promote sexual sin, it's easier to stay focused on Christ.

Step 4: Be Willing to Accept That There Is Life After, "No!"

❧ Your Reflection Pool ❧

This wasn't an easy reality for me to accept, but I had to do it: there is life after "no." If that man leaves because you've decided to honor the Almighty through a vow of celibacy, what more is there to say? How will that tarnish your future life of abundance? For the record, it won't . . . quite the opposite.

Step 5: Read *The Unwed Life: Survival Guide*

Read materials that strengthen your faith and determination to live a peaceful and pure life. The good news is that there are many good reads out today. One that I'd like to recommend is *Celibacy and Soul* by Susan J. Pollard. Another excellent resource is *6 Years and Counting* by Ashley M. Bennett.

And I'm excited to share that I've created *The Unwed Life: Survival Guide,* due out in 2020. This devotional is designed to help today's Christian single stay spiritually sane and focused in our modern, upside-down world. For more information about my upcoming books, please log on to www.tashmawhite.com.

Points to Remember

❒ Our Heavenly Father is bigger than our circumstance, even when we break our vow of celibacy.

❒ If we do happen to fall, we can get back up and embrace a life that will bring honor, not hurt, to our Heavenly Father.

❒ There are intentional steps we can take that will help us keep our focus during our vow of celibacy.

❒ When our love for the Messiah is bigger than our personal desire, we'll be able to thrive in a celibate lifestyle.

Finished Reading Chapter 8? ***Collect Your 8th Red Diamond.***

The world would have us to believe that a life of celibacy is not humanly possible. But anything is possible when we direct our focus at pleasing God.

9

The Fresh Scent of Forgiveness

"Sin gives us the stench of death, but the blood of Jesus Christ washes us with the fresh scent of forgiveness."

—Tashma White

Save for the road, I was completely surrounded by trees, with nothing but the moonlight to guide my footsteps. My head ached from the force of my teeth chattering together. I was paralyzed with fear and anxiously tried to guess the source of every sound I could hear coming from the nearby woods. The leaves on the trees danced from left to right as if the harsh wind were an instructor.

My toes began to throb as muddy water seeped into my shoes. I stared at my cold and soggy feet, trying to will them to become dry again. My gaze traveled slowly upward from my feet to my calves, continuing to my thighs, chest, and finally shoulders. I was completely covered with filth.

Where did all this dirt come from? I frantically thought.

Not sure of where I was going, I knew I had to find shelter soon. Silently I prayed, *Lord Jesus . . . please help me find somewhere safe and warm tonight!*

I resumed my journey down the road on painfully numb feet. With each step I took, it felt like hundreds of tiny needles piercing the

❧ Your Reflection Pool ❧

surface of my toes and heels. Suddenly, I noticed a white, tidy house about a hundred yards ahead. A warm glow from within illuminated a patch of the yard like a lighthouse guiding a shipwrecked passenger to shore.

Once I reached the home, I saw that the front porch light was on—as if someone expected company. I briefly hesitated, wiping the icy water and wet hair out of my eyes, then crept forward. But I couldn't bring myself to knock.

I stood there trembling like an abandoned puppy yearning for a loving Master. Suddenly, the door opened, and I heard a voice from within: *"Tashma, enter my gates with praise."* Astonished, it dawned on me that the voice hadn't called me "Tasha"—my nickname since I was six months old—but Tashma, my birth name (pronounced Taj-Ma). Whoever had called out, really knew me.

Gingerly, I went up the brick steps, opened the screen door, and walked in. I recognized the surroundings immediately: it was my great-grandmother's cozy, old-fashioned home. I grew up in that house and would have known it anywhere. It still had her white, narrow stove, and a sink with a longneck faucet accompanied by two small twist knobs for the hot and cold water. The round kitchen table, crowned by a red linoleum-covered top, stood on thin metal legs with matching chairs.

I moved in slow motion. It was as if some unknown force wanted me to slow down to fully grasp what I was seeing and experiencing. In a trance-like state, I turned left and looked inside Grandma's old bedroom. There they were: the same 1950s-style twin oak beds, adorned with her handmade, multicolored quilts. It must have taken me twenty seconds just to complete the ten steps into the room. Inside the large stone fireplace, a roaring fire burned—with no wood. I blinked several times to ensure that I wasn't hallucinating.

But before I could proceed further, a majestic voice addressed me from the blazing flames.

"My beloved daughter, I've waited so long for you to come to Me," said the magnificent voice that faded in and out. "Come," it beckoned. "Take off your shoes, for you stand on holy ground."

Never in a million years would I have guessed that I would be having my very own Moses encounter! Once I obeyed the command, the voice spoke again. "*Come*." Instantly, my heart began to pound wildly in my chest—because I now recognized His voice. I had heard it many times throughout my life, but always in a still and quiet manner. When I was sad and lonely, it was He who comforted me. When I sinned and asked for forgiveness, it was He who said, "You are forgiven." When my feelings were hurt and I was mistreated, He assured me, "I will never forsake nor leave you."

I stood with stunned wonder and thought,

~ Your Reflection Pool ~

My goodness! as my frostbitten mind attempted to thaw.

"*Come*," I heard again. Instantly, my spirit confirmed that this powerful presence was the Spirit of my Lord and Savior Jesus Christ. "My God!" I said numbly. Overwhelmed, I let tears of shame spill down my cheeks. "This filth," I raised my hands up for His inspection, "it won't wash off of me! It's the residue of all my sins. Forgive me, Father. I am so dirty and ashamed." I bitterly wept. My legs suddenly gave out from underneath me, and I collapsed onto the hardwood floor.

"Tashma, I know how you feel about yourself. Now it is time for you to know how I feel about you," said the Lord of Hosts. Head meekly bowed, I listened with reverence. "Forgive me, Jesus, I am not worthy to even lift my head in Your presence," I trembled and whispered.

"I have waited so long for you to come to me, Tashma!" He repeated. "The one thing you sought from the world is a love that only I can give you. Now that you have come to me, I will heal you, my child. I created you for a heavenly purpose. Use your testimony to draw others who are hurting worldwide into an embrace of forgiveness. The blood that I shed on Cavalry is the stain remover for any blemish of sin. Once My children are born again, they will have the fresh scent of eternal forgiveness."

"Jesus, I have made so many mistakes. All I ever wanted was someone to love me for me," I sobbed.

"I AM all that you desire in this life and beyond, Tashma. I AM the love and acceptance you have so desperately sought in others. Be strong and courageous, Tashma, I will never forsake nor leave you."

Slowly, I became aware that I was waking up—out of the dream. "Father, please don't leave me!" I desperately rose on my knees and begged. As my consciousness began to take over, He again promised, "Be strong and courageous. I will never forsake nor leave you, Tashma!"

I frantically yelled out, "Father, please . . . I need you!"

His voice drifted away like smoke evaporating in the air. "Be strong and courageous. I will never forsake nor leave you, Tashma!"

I can't tell you how many times I've thought on this dream. It has brought me comfort and courage—and it connects directly to the book you're holding in your hands. Partly through my dream, and partly through other events in my life, I know God commissioned me to write this book to enlighten women and girls who are walking or have walked in my shoes. What was our sin? We simply gave too much to men and boys who were not our wedded spouses. As a result, the Lord could not acknowledge an ordained connection between them and us. If our relationships were not authorized by Him, our Heavenly Father, how

❧ Your Reflection Pool ❧

can we settle for them?

In urging you not to become an "unwed wife," I'm not saying we should be disrespectful to our boyfriends or fiancés. We should always be honoring, and we should occasionally demonstrate the qualities of a good future wife to them. We should not, however, give them more authority or power than they deserve until they become our husband. When we do, it hinders our sacred relationship with the Great "I Am That I Am." Thank goodness, there is hope, along with God's heavenly instructions in His Holy Word, which will direct us back to Him if we fall.

Romans 12:2 tells us, "Do not conform any longer to the pattern of this world, but be transformed by the renewing of your mind. Then you will be able to test and approve

what God's will is—his good, pleasing and perfect will."

As believers, we must remember that we serve a jealous God who will not allow anyone or anything before Him. As long as we are lined up with the Word of God and keep Him first, we are on the right track. Ever notice how in a race, each runner must begin at the starting line? If they are not lined up properly or they run out of bounds, they are disqualified. This is symbolic of our life as a Christian. We are striving to make it to the finish line. When we sin, we are disqualified. The good news is when we get out of bounds, Jesus's sacrifice enables us to start the race again in order to finish the race to heaven. We are able to repent and begin once more. Galatians 5:1 says, "It is for freedom that Christ has set us free. Stand firm, then, and do not let yourselves be burdened again by a yoke of slavery."

I liken God's forgiveness to washing a load of laundry. Just like a soiled piece of clothing, our sins become stains on our spirit. When a garment becomes dirty, we place it into a washing machine. When the stench of our sins becomes too overpowering, we can go to God's throne of mercy to be washed clean. The blood that Jesus Christ shed on Cavalry is our washing detergent, which whitens our soul. The baptism of water is our rinse cycle; thankfully, we only have to get baptized once in a lifetime—God will still cleanse us whenever we come to Him for forgiveness. Repentance is our dryer, and the Holy Spirit becomes the fabric softener. When we are redeemed, the scent of the Holy Spirit permeates through us. This is how we receive the fresh scent of forgiveness! Like a baby who recognizes his mother's scent, our spirit is drawn to our Heavenly Father.

Satan and his demons can also smell our Father's fragrance on us. The evil devourer will then know we no longer belong to him. *Don't believe me?* The Word says in 2 Corinthians 2:14–16a: "But thanks be to God, who always leads us in triumphal procession in Christ and through us spreads everywhere the fragrance of the knowledge of Him. For we are to God the aroma of Christ among those who are being

❧ Your Reflection Pool ❧

saved and those who are perishing. To the one we are the smell of death; to the other, the fragrance of life."

So my darling sibling in Christ, let's promise ourselves: NO MORE UNWED WIFE! We were simply created for more . . . for greater! I pray this book, through the Holy Spirit, has enlightened you as to why it's simply not worth it to be out of God's will.

The truth is, dating can be a wonderful and joyous experience. It can lead us to courtship and to marriage in ways that are God-honoring and life-giving for us and for the men in our lives. It is my fervent prayer that when we date, we'll do it with a spiritual mindset.

Points to Remember

❐ Just like a soiled piece of clothing, our sins become stains on our spirit.

❐ When the stench of our sins becomes too overpowering, we can go to God's throne of mercy to be washed clean.

❒ The blood that Jesus Christ shed on Cavalry is our washing detergent, which whitens our soul.

Finished Reading Chapter 9? ***Collect Your 9th Red Diamond.***

When we are redeemed, the scent of the Holy Spirit permeates through us.

A Final Note

In case you may need a little help and/or encouragement along the way, I have included two appendices of prayers written for single women and young ladies in any circumstance they may find themselves in. You will find them after this page. A Glossary of Terms at the back of this book has been provided for further clarification and assistance. I pray this tool, indeed the entire book, will serve as a helpful resource to you. May our Lord keep you now and forever, in the name of Jesus Christ, Amen.

- Want Tashma to host a *Women's Singles* seminar for your women's retreat or singles ministry?
- Interested in having her attend your next book club meeting via a thirty-minute Skype session?

For more information - visit www.Tashmawhite.com

A Word of Thanks for You

Thank you so much for traveling through the passages of this book with me! I pray God surrounds you with peace, protection, prosperity, grace, and mercy. May your life be filled with wisdom, purpose, passion, and the guidance of the Holy Spirit. If you would kindly pray that the Holy Spirit will continually guide me with the clarity of God's will for me, I would humbly be most grateful. May God's redemption encamp around you with eternal blessings. In the name of Jesus Christ, I declare and decree this prayer for you all the days of your life! Amen. *Selah!*

Your Sister-In-Christ,

Tashma White

Appendix A: Prayers for Today's Single Woman

i.

A Prayer for the Sister Who Wants to Break the Curse of *The Unwed Wife Syndrome*

Lord Jesus, I have read this book and now recognize that I've been an unwed wife. I ask You to strengthen me to stand firm and withstand any temptation. Father, please bind my thoughts to Your will for my life. Teach me how to fully live to please You, Omnipotent God. I need You to help me, Lord, because I know I cannot do this thing by myself! Please never leave me nor forsake me, Precious Father. Hold my hand and guide me every step of the way. I want to live a life that brings honor to Your Holy Name. Teach me how to conduct myself as a single woman of God at home, around my friends, at work, and on dates. Forgive me for choosing my needs over Yours, Merciful Savior. I ask these things in the exalted name of Jesus Christ. *Amen. Selah!*

ii.

The Red Diamond (No Unwed Wife) Pledge

On this day _____ of _________ 20___ I,

____

___, commit to live my life henceforth in a way that truly honors my Lord and Savior, Jesus Christ. I will do this in reverence to Him who died for my sins. This is why I am now committing to a vow of celibacy. This is one way in which my private life will line up with my public life as a daughter of Jesus Christ. Precious Lord, guide me so that I will be able to keep this holy vow. It is not my intent to ever fail myself, or most importantly, You! Please bless me with the desire to stay faithful to this pledge. I commit to not having sex until I am a married woman. Teach me how to stay focused in this cause. Show me how to date from a spiritual perspective instead of a worldly one. In the name of Jesus Christ I pray, *Amen. Selah!*

iii.

A Prayer for the Sister Who Lacks Self-Awareness

Heavenly Father, I admit that I suffer from a lack of self-awareness. Show me who I am in the body of Christ. Teach me how to behave as a woman who draws her confidence and strength from You, not from the things of the world.

Precious Father, teach me who I am meant to be in Jesus Christ. Help me to discover the true essence of ______________________________ (*fill in your name*). I want to know my true purpose and role in Your kingdom building plan. Please reveal to me an awareness of who I am and why I am here. My Lord, please bless me with a hunger for your Word and a never-ending desire to do Your will. In the name of Jesus Christ I pray, *Amen. Selah!*

iv.

A Prayer for the Sister Who Lacks Self-Respect

Gracious Lord, I can finally confess that I suffer from a lack of self-respect. This has been one of the hardest self-discoveries I have ever made. I want every aspect of my life to show that I am a respectful and respectable woman of God. I will demonstrate this through my dress, speech, and behavior, both personally and professionally. As a daughter of Jesus Christ, I am obligated to conduct myself as a lady of virtue. I am a child of the King of Kings and the Lord of Lords; therefore, teach me to appreciate my own individuality, body, and mind. May both my private and public life draw others to Christ and build Your kingdom. In the name of Jesus Christ I pray, *Amen. Selah!*

v.

A Prayer for the Sister Who Lacks Self-Worth

My God, please enlighten me to my own self-worth. Give me the desire to study and comprehend Your Word so I can fully understand whom I belong to in Jesus Christ. Please destroy my strongholds due to a lack of self-worth. I want to know my worth in the Lord. It is to You, Heavenly Father, that I will look and discover who I truly am and all that I am purposed to be in this world. Create in me a new life worth living and self-assurance that the world cannot take away. In the name of Jesus

Christ I pray, *Amen. Selah!*

vi.

A Prayer for the Sister Who Has A Fear of Being Alone

Merciful Father, I know You created me to live a life of fulfillment. However, I have been in bondage to a fear of being alone. This is why I've settled for the past relationships that I've been in. This stronghold has also been a hindrance in other areas of my life. For instance, at times I've put up with fake friends who are a negative influence in my life. All of that just so I won't be by myself and have no one to talk with. Please, Lord, deliver me from this crippling oppression. I want to experience everything that You have for me in this lifetime. I am aware that I cannot do this if I am limited by self-inflicted fear. Destroy this hindrance in me, Precious Savior. For the first time in my life, I willingly lay this burden down and claim in Jesus's name that I will never take it up again.

All praises to You, Holy Father. In the name of Jesus Christ I pray, *Amen. Selah!*

vii.

A Prayer for the Sister Who Has A Fear of Rejection

Omnipotent God, I confess that I suffer from a fear of rejection. This has affected my life in more ways than one. Whether this fear began in my childhood or adult life, I pray You will deliver me from it. Please, Lord, I no longer want to be bound by this stronghold. Please help me to remember that my Heavenly Father rules over the highest of all kingdoms, far greater than any man-made thrones. May the knowledge of Your love and presence nurture my self-assurance henceforward. Therefore, I proclaim in Jesus's name, that I will never feel unloved or unwanted again. May I draw all my strength, courage, and self-acceptance from my Lord and Savior. In the name of Jesus Christ I pray, *Amen. Selah!*

viii.

A Prayer for the Sister Who Wants to Give Her Life to the Lord

Most Gracious Father, I humbly confess that I am a sinner and that I've been living a "have it my way" lifestyle. I repent of all my sins and disobedience to Your Word. I admit that I need You in my life! Teach me Your ways, sweet Jesus. I acknowledge You as my God, Creator of Heaven and Earth, Holy Messiah. Please mend all of my broken pieces, Magnificent Lord! Purge and prune all my carnal ways. I surrender my life to You, Glorious Creator. I confess that I am a sinner; I have sinned against You and Your Holy Throne. I believe in my heart that Jesus Christ is Your Son and that You sent Your Son to earth, he was born of a virgin and that He was crucified for my sins so that I might have eternal life. I believe Jesus knew no sin and bore not only my sins but the sins of all mankind. I believe Jesus rose after three days from a borrowed tomb with all power in His hand. I believe He will return again to escort all repentant believers to heaven.

Lord, I need to know You for myself, not just from what others say about You. Give me the desire to study Your Word and apply it to my everyday life. Teach me how to please You, Lord. I need You to be the rock upon which I now stand, no matter what happens in my life! Teach me how to listen and be obedient to Your voice. I repent of all my sins, as well as choose to follow and obey Jesus Christ as my personal Lord and Savior. I'm now ready to walk into my purpose, but I need You and the guidance of the Holy Counselor to lead me. Heavenly Father, please fill me with the presence of the Holy Spirit and use my life as a willing vessel for building Your kingdom. I now walk in complete faith, knowing that I belong to the Most High God.

Should I lose my life today, I am at peace with knowing that I will be with You in Heaven. Guide me to a Bible-teaching church led by a true servant of God. I humbly ask this and all things in the name of Jesus Christ, my personal Lord and Savior. Amen. *Selah*

ix.

A Prayer for the Sister Who Wants to Be Married Someday

Precious Lord and Savior, please hear Your daughter's prayer. Father, I humbly come to Your throne of grace and mercy asking You to bless me with my destined mate. Lord, you know I *do not* just want any piece of man! I want a man who is in a life-serving, fully committed relationship with You, Father. A man who has spiritual wisdom and honors You with his obedience, finances, talents, gifts, and time. I do not want satan's counterfeit, Lord Jesus! I only desire that man who was tailor-made for me, by You. Sweet Jesus, please open my spiritual eyes of discernment. I want only what You have for me, Lord God. Block any wolves in sheep's clothing from even approaching me.

I see other happy couples, and I want that for myself and much more. Please bless me with the patience to wait on You, Lord, and not jump ahead of Your divine plan for my life. Please continue Your work in me so that I will be ready when You reveal my future husband to me.

Almighty Creator, until such time I pray he will not be bound by any sexual perversions. I also pray he will not succumb to any addiction, double-mindedness, gambling, mental disorders, procrastination, selfishness, laziness, joblessness, or disrespectful mindsets. Father, let him be a smart worker in his career and willing to work to build Your kingdom. I pray he will be strong enough to lead and wise enough to know when to follow. Lord, let him not be a man of foolish pride, but honorable and secure in his manhood. I pray he will faithfully tithe and be a good steward over what You have blessed him with in life. May he also have an appreciative, respectful, and considerate spirit toward me and my family. In the name of Jesus

Christ I declare and decree this prayer. In the name of Jesus Christ I pray, *Amen. Selah!*

x.

A Prayer for the Sister Who Keeps Choosing Mr. Wrong

Holy God, I confess that my judgment regarding men is not wise. I keep picking the bad apple out of the bushel! Gracious Lord, please help me end this vicious cycle right now. Heal any spiritual and emotional wounds that have caused me to keep choosing Mr. Wrong. Teach me to draw closer to You so that I will develop a mature spirit of discernment regarding men. I know there are some good men out there, but I need Your guidance in order to recognize the right one. Let him be a doer of the Holy Word, not just a talker. Please bless me with the patience to wait on You this time, Lord God! Prevent me from giving into my emotions or feelings of loneliness so that I will not repeat my past mistakes. Keep me, Loving Father, away from any counterfeit mates; I only want my destined one. Lord, I surrender my will to Your will so that I can truly hear from You the next time. Forgive me for leaning on my own understanding and not Yours. I ask the Holy Spirit to come into my life so that I can learn from my past mistakes. In the magnificent name of Jesus Christ, I pray. *Amen. Selah!*

xi.

A Prayer for the Single Mother Who Longs for a Loving and Faithful Man of God

Heavenly Father, I come to you today asking You to hear my sincere prayer. I ask the Holy Spirit to overflow in my life and guide me in how to be a virtuous mother. Let me always be mindful that my child(ren) are watching me. You have blessed me, Most Gracious Father; let me never abuse my gift as a mother. Teach me to how to nurture my children with love and patience, as well as raise them to be respectful, God-fearing individuals. I pray that I will not fall prey to any wolves in sheep's clothing. Lord, please teach me to wait on the man You have destined to be my husband, provider to my family, and nurturing father to my child(ren). Please let him be a man who is respectful, honorable, patient, caring, thoughtful, wise, tastefully funny, responsible, a good steward of your blessings, a tither, unselfish, loving, and full of integrity. Most importantly, let him be a man who lives by the Word of God. In the name of Jesus Christ I pray, *Amen. Selah!*

xii.

A Prayer for the Sister Who Is Struggling With Her Finances[1]

Eternal Father, as you are already aware, I confess that I am struggling with my finances. This has become an emotional strain on me, and I can't bare it any longer. Your Word tells us in

---

[1] A great resource for the deliverance from debt is a book by Michelle Singletary entitled, *The 21-Day Financial Fast: Your Path to Financial Peace and Freedom.* I personally received several financial breakthroughs with this biblically based plan of action.

Proverbs 22:7b that "the borrower is the slave to the lender." Lord, my expenses far outweigh my income. If truth be told, I am addicted to shopping because it temporarily fills a hollow within me. However, the more I get, the more I need! As your daughter, I am aware that Your Word and presence should be the only hungers that I crave. Creator of all things, please deliver me from this stronghold, and I pray that my future husband won't be bound by the same addiction. Heal the hole in my spirit that exists in me, Messiah. Luke 12:15 says, "Take care, and be on your guard against all covetousness, for one's life does not consist in the abundance of his possessions." Please Heavenly Father, teach me how to live a life without coveting worldly possessions.

Prayers of Healing

A Prayer of Healing for the Divorced Sister in Christ

Only You truly know the circumstances that

drove me to a divorce. Only You can see what the world cannot. Therefore, only You can judge me for it. I ask for forgiveness, healing, and restoration from this life-changing event. Please teach me how to truly wait on You the next time so that I don't have to travel down this painful road again. I pray You will cleanse my spirit of anything that would prevent me from having a meaningful, anointed, equally yoked and fulfilled marriage the next time. I ask that You increase my spiritual discernment. In addition, give me the obedience to heed the warning signs that the Holy Spirit reveals to me when I am dating next time so that I don't fall for the wrong relationship again. I fully submit myself to Your will for my life and claim my healing. In the mighty name of Jesus, I most humbly pray. Amen! Selah!

A Prayer of Healing for the Sister Who Is Having Suicidal Thoughts

Holy Creator, You know my weaknesses

and strengths. You know what I hide in the secret crevices of my heart. You see what the world cannot. Lord, I confess that I've been feeling like life just isn't worth living anymore. I know this is a trick of the enemy! That's why, Father, I am begging You to please heal me from this demonic stronghold. Furthermore, I believe every one of Your children has a purpose for his or her life. However, I have no clue what mine is! Shower me with Your anointed presence and unwavering peace. Teach me who I am in You and lead me to a life of purposeful living. In the everlasting name of Jesus, I pray. Amen! Selah!

A Prayer of Healing and Restoration for the Sister Who Has Been a Victim of Domestic Abuse

Merciful Father, I have a secret; one that You already know about. Almighty God, I am ashamed to confess before You that I am a victim of domestic abuse. I still can't believe how in the world I got here! I desperately need healing from this toxic relationship. It has taken from me far more than I ever received. That's why, Beloved Protector, I'm asking for your deliverance, healing, and restoration. You created me to live a life that brings You honor, not one that forces me to cower in fear, hurt, and shame. Please heal the invisible wounds that keep me cocooned in low self-esteem, uncertainty, and emotional sewage. Give me protection, a safe place, financial resources, strength, desire, and courage to break free from the shackles of degradation. Lord, You are the Author and Finisher of my faith. Please bless me with a new, amazing chapter of transformation for me (and my children). In the majestic name of Jesus, I most humbly and faithfully pray. Amen! Selah!

A Prayer of Healing for the Sister Who Has Been Sexually Abused

Eternal Savior, as You well know, there is a dark secret from my past that has kept me bound in hurt and shame, even up to today. Lord, Your Word tells us that our body is a sacred temple. But Father, what happens when our temple becomes violated? Lord, growing up, I could never have imagined that I would be sexually molested! If truth be told, for the longest time, I blamed You for this unfair violation. Now, I want to confess my anger and bitterness to You and ask for Your forgiveness, Almighty King. I desperately need Your presence and love in my life. Holy Messiah, I beg you to please heal me from this emotionally draining trauma! I know You are a God of Love, not hurt and pain. I want to be released from this stronghold, once and for all. Dear Lord, please lead me to the right resources that will help sustain my healing and deliverance. Please show me through Your Word how to live a life of freedom, joy, forgiveness, and peace. Furthermore, if it's Your will, Mighty Deliverer, please reveal a path of purpose to me that will allow me to use my testimony to help heal others. In the everlasting name of Jesus

Christ, I most faithfully pray. Amen! Selah!

Appendix B:

Prayers for Today's Young Lady

i.

A Prayer for the Young Lady Who Wants to Break the Curse of The Unwed Wife Syndrome

Lord Jesus, I have read this book and now recognize that I've been an unwed wife. I ask

You to strengthen me to stand firm and withstand any temptation. Father, please bind my thoughts to Your will for my life. Teach me how to fully live to please You, Omnipotent God. I need You to help me, Lord, because I know I cannot do this thing by myself! Please never leave nor forsake me, Precious Father. Hold my hand and guide me every step of the way. I want to live a life that brings honor to Your Holy Name. Teach me how to conduct myself as a single woman of God at home, around my friends, at work, and on dates. Forgive me for choosing my needs over Yours, Merciful Savior. I ask these things in the exalted name of Jesus Christ. *Amen. Selah!*

ii.

The *Red Diamond* (No Unwed Wife) Pledge

On this day _____ of _________ 20___ I,

____,

commit to live my life henceforth in a way that truly honors my Lord and Savior, Jesus Christ. I will do this in reverence to Him who died for my sins. This is why I am now committing to a vow of celibacy and even more importantly, obedience. This is one way in which my private life will line up with my public life as a daughter of Jesus Christ. Precious Lord, guide me so that I will be able to keep this holy vow. It is not my intent to ever fail myself, or most importantly, You! Please bless me with the desire to stay faithful to this pledge. I commit to not having sex until I am a married woman. Teach me how to stay focused in this cause. Show me how to date from a spiritual perspective instead of a worldly one. In the name of Jesus Christ I pray, *Amen. Selah!*

iii.

A Prayer for the Young Lady Just Beginning to Date

Heavenly Father, I am a young lady with her whole life ahead of her. Please teach me how to live in a way that honors You. I do not want to make the same mistakes that others have made regarding men. Humbly I ask You to show me, Lord, how to live only for You. Father, I do not want to make decisions today that will lead to a life full of regrets. Give me a desire to date like a respectable young lady of Christ. I am aware that I can never regain the days of my youth once they are gone. Therefore, Lord, please bless me to live wisely, with a mindset to gain an education and a positive work ethic that will benefit me for the rest of my life. Please give me the courage not to settle on the wrong guy. I pray that You will give me the desire to want to enrich my life in Your fullness. Please help me to realize that the decision to marry is a serious one and that I must not take it lightly. Until such time, please allow me to live as a virtuous young lady with a promising and purposeful future. In the name of Jesus Christ, I pray, *Amen. Selah!*

iv.

A Prayer for the Young Lady Who Is Going Off to College

Sovereign God, I am going off to college, and I really don't know what all to expect. Father, please allow me to make the most out of this blessed opportunity. It's not enough just to go, but I want to complete my education. Lord, I'm a saved young lady living in a sinful and unforgiving world. I do not want to look back on these promising years of my life with regret due to mistakes that I made while in college. So please, Father, give me a mind to stay focused, a heart for Your presence, discernment to detect bad influences, fortitude to avoid them, and an ear to listen to the guidance of the Holy Spirit. Please help me to fully understand that every action I take will bring either a positive or a negative consequence. Precious Lord, give me the wisdom not to be my own worst "enemy in the mirror." Please give me the courage to live a life both privately and publicly as an obedient daughter of the Most High God. In the name of Jesus I pray, *Amen. Selah!*

v.

A Prayer for the Young Lady Who Is in School or College

Lord, I realize these are supposed to be some of the best years of my life. Please help me to operate on a path moving forward that will allow me to receive the prize of my education. Most Gracious Father, please give me the desire to always carry myself in a respectful manner that will make my family proud of me. Forgive me, Lord, for the mistakes I may have committed up to this point in my life. I repent of all my sins in the name of Jesus. Teach me how to present myself as an *heiress to His throne*. Please bless me with the mind of a leader who rises above peer pressure. Please bless me with a desire to study and stay in Your Word. Help me find and bond with other Christian students here on campus. Bless me with positive and focused friends who are likeminded in their desire to study and to follow You. Help me to discern the users or those who would take advantage of me. Holy Spirit, please give me the courage to do what's right in the eyes of the Lord. I do not want to be known as some guy's plaything or trick. I desire to be considered a young woman of class, who is marriage material in God's ways. In Jesus Christ's name I pray these and all things. *Amen. Selah!*

vi.

A Prayer for the Unmarried Young Lady Who Has Children

Precious Lord, You are a forgiving God. As You know, I have a child (or children), but I am not married. Your Word warns us not to judge so that we will not be judged in return. My Lord, forgive those who have sat in judgment of me for getting pregnant without a husband. I ask this on their behalf, because I pray You will completely forgive me for all the sins that I have committed in my lifetime. Please bless my child and protect him/her with Your dedicated angels. Jesus, please keep him/her even when I have left this world. Teach me to raise my child in a household that is not led by a woman with an unwed wife mindset. My children deserve better than that! Let me always be mindful of how I conduct myself as a godly woman. Show me how to be a positive and nurturing mother to my children. In the name of Jesus Christ I pray these and all things. *Amen. Selah!*

Your Reflection Pool

❧ Your Reflection Pool ❧

Glossary of Terms

Appetizer-Style Woman (ASW)—This woman captures a solid hold of her man at the beginning of the relationship by stimulating his interest. Unfortunately, she only whets his appetite, never quite satisfying it. She simply holds him over until what he really wants comes along.

Beloved—A term of endearment for any reader of this book. ☺

Blemish—A mark or imperfection that spoils an appearance. Something that spoils a person's reputation or good record.

Born Again—A spiritual rebirth that each Christian experiences upon their conversion of faith in the belief and acceptance of Jesus Christ as their personal savior and His crucifixion for the forgiveness of our sins.

Carnal—Sensual or sexual

Christian Sociopath—Someone who has no remorse or conscience when they are disobedient to God's Word.

Codes of Conduct—Behaviors that single daughters of Jesus Christ should strive to implement in their lives.

Common-Law Wife—A woman who has lived with a man for years with the "intent to be married" or performs as a wife although unmarried.

Common—Often occurring or frequently seen; without special privilege, rank, or status

Counterfeit—An imposter. This is a man who has stolen the identity of your destined mate. He looks and talks like the man with whom you were intended to share your life, but you later find out he was simply a counterfeit. A duplicate or copy from a mold of any man, not the original man that God intended for you.

Courting—To spend time together in a romantic relationship as a prelude to getting married.

Dating—Spending time with someone for casual and/or entertainment purposes.

Daughter of Jesus Christ—A woman or young lady who has committed her life to serving our Heavenly Father and Lord Jesus Christ.

"Desperately Seeking Male" Type of Woman —A woman who believes it's better to have a piece of a man than no man at all.

Dessert-Style Woman (DSW) —A woman who suffocates her man through clinginess and insecurity. Ultimately, pushing him away because of her need for constant attention.

Destined Mate—A man whom the Lord has custom-made just for you. Furthermore, God has a divinely appointed time for him to meet you.

Dignity—A proper sense of pride and self-respect or the condition of being worthy of respect, esteem, or honor.

Down Low Brother—A male who openly dates women but secretly sleeps with other men.

Enemy—Someone whose aim is to sabotage your future goals and inspirations; a person who does not have your best interest at heart; a person whose influence will damage your integrity and reputation.

El Shaddai—God Almighty

E-WAR Hustle—Engaged Without A Ring. A hustle that men play with a woman they've shown no real intent to marry.

Fruits of the Spirit—Based on Galatians 5:22. These are the characteristics that distinguish children of God from the world: "But the fruit of the Spirit is love, joy, peace, patience, kindness, goodness, faithfulness, gentleness and self-control."

Full-Course-Meal Woman (FCMW)—This woman has multiple aspects to her life. This secure lady has much to offer while also having her own interests and hobbies. Her love interest is not overwhelmed with trying to be her only source for happiness. Her life is lined up with the will of God. In addition, she diligently seeks the Heavenly Father's leading in all she does.

Giving the Wrong Impression (GTWI) – Behavior that encourages people to question the sincerity of our walk with Jesus. It often leads to public disgrace and spiritual self-sabotage.

Godly Self-Love—Understanding your value in Jesus Christ.

H.I.M. —Husband-in-Marriage. A husband through the means of marriage, not due to shacking or because he is your baby daddy.

Holy Ghost–filled man—A man whose actions reflect the guidance of the Holy Spirit. An honorable man who leans not on his own understanding but that of the Lord. He applies the Word of God to every aspect of his daily life.

Holy Ghost–filled woman—A woman whose actions reflect the guidance of the Holy Spirit. An honorable woman who leans not on her own understanding but that of the Lord. She applies the Word of God to every aspect of her daily life.

Holy Spirit—In Christianity, the third person of the Trinity, understood as the spiritual force of God. Often referred to as the voice of God. As Corrie Huyser once wrote, "the Holy Spirit joins our mind to the Mind of God so we are able to hear Him."

Honor—A place of distinction, recognition, and privilege.

Idol—A person, place, or thing that is used as an object of worship.

Insanity—Performing the same action over and over again while expecting a different result.

Lady—One who is gracious, polite, hospitable, and dignified; not arrogant, rude, or having a sense of entitlement.

Like—to be fond of.

Long-term shacking—Living with a man who is not our husband for the purpose of being lovers.

Marriage—A legally recognized relationship, established by a civil or religious ceremony, between a man and woman who intend to live together as sexual partners.

Movement—A collective effort by a large number of people to try to achieve something, especially a political, religious, or social change.

Proverbs 31 Woman—A humble, noble, and virtuous woman who is obedient to the Word of God and lives a life to brings honor unto the Lord as well as her family.

Redeemed—Restored to favor or forgiveness.

Revolution—Dramatic change in ideas or practice.

Selah—An ancient Hebrew word. Most Jewish scholars agree that it means "forever."

Shacking—A woman sharing the same room with a man who is not her husband for the purpose of an intimate or sexual relationship.

Short-term Shacking—Temporarily staying with a man who is not our husband for the purpose of an intimate and/or sexual relationship, no matter how temporary the stay.

Single Woman—A woman who is unmarried or exhibits the characteristics of being unmarried. One who has yet to complete the sacrament of marriage.

Snack-Style Woman (SSW) —A woman who, once sampled, is easily forgotten. A man will think nothing of leaving her because his connection to her is only on a superficial basis. They may share sex, but they have no mutual emotional bond or commitment. When there's no emotional attachment, a man is less likely to treat you with respect.

Soul Tie—An ungodly spiritual link that is shared between two people after they have sex.

Stand-In Man—One who stands in the place of your true destined mate; one who has self-serving tendencies. Essentially, he has no intentions of ever getting marriage. He is a taker by nature, not a giver.

Stand-Up Man—One who stands up for his woman, particularly when she needs it most;

one whose actions show that he is a honorable man. A man of valor.

Syndrome—A group of things or events that form a recognizable pattern, especially of something undesirable. Also called a condition, disorder, or set of symptoms.

The Waiting Game—A mind game that we women choose to play with ourselves in the grand hopes that a particular man will eventually decide to settle down and marry us.

Unwed Wife—A woman who *consistently* performs the duties of a wife for a man she is not married to; thus, she has set the expectation that she will continue to do so while in a committed relationship with a man who is not her husband. *Symptoms may include cooking for a man on a regular basis, taking care of his sexual needs, shacking and/or creating a family together, playing mother to his biological child(ren).*

Unwed Wife Syndrome—A spiritual stronghold that blurs one's perception of how an unmarried daughter of Christ should share her life with a man who is not her husband.

Unequally Yoked Marriages—A marriage where the wife and husband are not spiritually lined up or equal. One is a spiritually minded believer of Jesus Christ while the other is not.

Wed—To marry in a formal ceremony; take as one's husband or wife. To bind by close or lasting ties; to become united or to blend.